METAETHICS
FROM A FIRST PERSON
STANDPOINT

Catherine Wilson is the Anniversary Professor of Philosophy at the University of York. Catherine has worked in the history of philosophy, moral theory and aesthetics and has taught and published extensively in these fields. Her publications include *A Very Short Introduction to Epicureanism, Epicureanism at the Origins of Modernity* (2008 and 2010), *Moral Animals: Ideals and Constraints in Moral Theory* (2004 and 2007) and (with C. Wilson and D. Clarke), *The Oxford Handbook of Philosophy in Early Modern Europe* (2011).

Metaethics from a First Person Standpoint

An Introduction to Moral Philosophy

Catherine Wilson

OpenBook Publishers

http://www.openbookpublishers.com

© 2016 Catherine Wilson

All external links were active on 08 January 2016 and have been archived via the Internet Archive Wayback Machine at https://archive.org/web

Updated digital material and resources associated with this volume are available at http://www.openbookpublishers.com/isbn/9781783741984#resources

ISBN Paperback: 978-1-78374-198-4
ISBN Hardback: 978-1-78374-199-1
ISBN Digital (PDF): 978-1-78374-200-4
ISBN Digital ebook (epub): 978-1-78374-201-1
ISBN Digital ebook (mobi): 978-1-78374-202-8
DOI: 10.11647/OBP.0087

Cover image: Nick Jewell, 'Tiree Perspective' (2008), CC BY 4.0. https://www.flickr.com/photos/macjewell/2736570618

All paper used by Open Book Publishers is SFI (Sustainable Forestry Initiative), PEFC (Programme for the Endorsement of Forest Certification Schemes) and Forest Stewardship Council(r)(FSC(r) certified.

Printed in the United Kingdom, United States, and Australia
by Lightning Source for Open Book Publishers (Cambridge, UK).

Dedicated to Caroline, Willy, and Harry,
my siblings—and friends for life.

Contents

Introduction

At every level of philosophical enquiry into moral theory, from the introductory to the advanced, the question of the objectivity or subjectivity of moral judgements resurfaces. Are there moral truths—or only opinions and beliefs? If there are such truths, how can we come to know them? Can one coherently deny that any moral opinion is better than any other? And could one simply turn one's back on morality and, if so, what would this involve?

Metaethics is the study of these and related questions. Unlike the practitioners of 'normative ethics,' the metaethicist need not take a position on what anyone may do, or ought to do or is forbidden to do, or on what is morally right or wrong. He or she is interested rather in how moral language and moral thought work, no matter what the contents of anyone's set of moral beliefs may be or what their practices amount to.

My aim in this book is to address the central questions of metaethics and to give serious answers to them. In writing it, I wanted to present a coherent and positive argument for the existence of moral knowledge that would be persuasive in the face of the possibility that morality is both a natural phenomenon and a human invention. At the same time, I was dissatisfied with many textbook presentations of the 'isms' of moral theory. It is all too easy to lose one's way in a forest of taxonomy and then to abandon all hope and fall back on dogmatism or nihilism. I had in mind a freer sort of enquiry and one that would decisively eliminate both of those options.

It occurred to me that there was a model that might prove useful. Facing an array of competing claims and systems, and saddled with a scholastic vocabulary that had long supported debate and discussion without answering any fundamental questions about the *world*, a philosopher had once responded by adopting, first, a posture of scepticism—indeed of hyperbolic doubt. Professing to reject all previous systems, he attempted to

    http://dx.doi.org/10.11647/OBP.0087.10

derive important results in ontology as well as an understanding of human epistemological competence by arguing in a strict linear fashion from his 'first-person' standpoint. Although there is much to dispute as well as to admire in his argumentation, Descartes's strategy is agreed to have paid off handsomely. So I resolved to attempt a similar strategy, inventing an Enquirer who, in a state of uncertainty and confusion, decides to adopt the assumption that nothing is really good or bad, obligatory or prohibited, and that there is no such thing as moral understanding or moral knowledge. My aim was then to explore this position, which I first extended into a radical scepticism about all values ascribed to a group called the Destroyers of Illusion, to see where it would lead and whether it would run into difficulties.

In considering this nihilistic position, my Enquirer discovers that the Destroyers have gone too far in their claim that we live in a value-free universe in which nothing about goodness and worth can be known. The Enquirer realises that she is motivated to pursue what's good for her and able to come to some firm conclusions regarding her own self-interest. She finds that she can also know, in some cases, what's good for other people whose situations she comes to understand. The Enquirer then turns to consider the topic of manners—the 'norms of civility.' These are social conventions specifying how two or more people in certain situations ought to treat one another. The Enquirer perceives that she mostly knows about and is mostly motivated to observe these norms, but that, as items of knowledge, these conventions have to be learned. Further, acting in a mannerly fashion is sometimes inconvenient or contrary to self-interest. The reasons for 'opting out' of a local system of what's considered good manners, on particular occasions or altogether, are explored. The Enquirer finally proceeds to consider morals—which, like manners, concern the interactions between two or more people and how they ought to treat one another. The similarities and differences between manners and morals are explored in terms of how they become items of knowledge, the motives for conforming to them, and the possible reasons for 'opting out' of morality either occasionally or completely.

In thus reasoning out metaethics from a first-person standpoint, the conclusions my Enquirer reaches are that moral claims are different to mere expressions of moral feelings and emotional reactions, though they are firmly tied to our individual and collective preferences; that there are good reasons both for remaining within the morality system and for sometimes rejecting norms accepted by the ambient culture. Further, my Enquirer discovers there is a tendency for moral knowledge to increase when no obstacles are put in its way, and that there is good sense in the notion that moral enquiry is aimed at the discovery of moral truths. There is plenty that is contentious in my construction, as there was in the model upon which it is loosely based, but I hope the line of reasoning can be defended, as well as challenged, by able students. My overall aim is that readers who have worked their way through the arguments will decisively set aside the more commonplace forms of scepticism and moral nihilism to which they would otherwise be inclined. Moral confidence, rather than moral certainty, is the epistemological aim.

In composing my text, I found that most of the major issues and concepts of metaethics, ranging from Plato's worries about the relationship between power and truth, Hume's account of the virtues, and Kant's universalisation thought-experiments to contemporary theorising about plans and motives, practical reasons, moral realism, and the Darwinian perspective on human social life were raised at one point or another. Rather than seeing these treatments as belonging to competing theories, I suggest they individually capture different elements of a large and complex picture of moral learning, moral communication, and the progress of moral knowledge. Here, data sources, ideas, and positions are referenced in the endnotes and in the chapter-by-chapter suggestions for further reading. I hope this will make my book useful in a second respect. I would encourage readers to follow up the references that interest them and to study some of the old and new classics of moral theory and metaethics before, during, or after their encounter with the present text.

Though grammarians will wince at each occurrence, I have occasionally used 'they,' 'their,' and 'them' for the singular in order to maintain gender neutrality.

Acknowledgements

I am grateful to the undergraduate and postgraduate students of Rice University, Houston, Texas and the University of York (UK) who worked their way through earlier drafts of the manuscript. Special thanks are due as well to my referees with their many suggestions for improvement.

Enquiry I

The Enquirer finds that the moral opinions and practices of mankind form a confusing jumble in which, while strong convictions reign, it is hard to see why any moral claims can claim to be true or to be known by anyone. She decides to doubt everything she has assumed hitherto about moral good and moral evil and her understanding of them.

Tot homines, quot opiniones — as many opinions as men! as the saying goes. Ever since I came to know something of the wider world, I have been curious about the variety of beliefs and practices that human beings have accepted and engaged in. I have been impressed by their variety but also sometimes troubled by their character.

Many of the things people do from time to time for the sake of others strike me as noble and heroic. Firemen rush into burning buildings to save the lives of children and animals. Reporters travel to battle zones in war-torn countries to inform the world about what is happening there. Politicians defy opposition to demand civil rights for disfavoured groups, and middle-class people sacrifice luxuries to send their children to school or to donate to famine relief. In ordinary life, people go out of their way to help friends and even strangers, giving each other rides to the airport, assisting with the dishwashing, cheering up the depressed and calming the anxious amongst them.

Yet just as many of the things people sometimes do seem cruel and shocking, and this has been noted and lamented by philosophers for centuries. For thousands of years, people have enslaved their fellow humans to build walls and palaces, to weave textiles, and to farm their fields.[1] Now they are enslaved to manufacture sportswear and electronic equipment. From my readings, I have learned that torture was acceptable judicial practice throughout the 17th century, and that only a few hundred years ago in Europe, a criminal could be publically hanged, disembowelled,

 http://dx.doi.org/10.11647/OBP.0087.01

drawn and quartered. I know that cockfights and bullfights have been considered amusing by many cultures and that ancient people would cut slabs of flesh off their living cattle to eat.[2] Massacres and child armies are widespread in the contemporary world, as is sex trafficking. The newspaper brings constant reports of corrupt police officers and politicians. I have read that the ancient Greeks, with their brilliant mathematicians, poets, and sculptors, left their unwanted babies on the hillside to die or to be picked up and raised by strangers.[3] Detailed reports of the abuse of children and old people in nurseries, orphanages, and care homes hit the papers on an alarmingly regular basis. It seems their caretakers, or some of them anyway, think that what they are doing is absolutely fine.

I suspect that future generations will look back at some of our current practices—perhaps the prison system, factory farming, and the treatment of workers in the garment industry–with the same disapproval with which we look back on the flogging of sailors and draft animals, the slave trade, the mutilation of women's feet, and the guillotine. Many of these practices and institutions have been abandoned in parts of the world in which they were formerly common. But did people discover that there were human rights nobody had known about before? Will people of the future discover more rights—perhaps the rights of plants, landscapes, or insects—in addition to 'human rights' and 'animal rights'? Could we decide some day in the distant future that we were actually mistaken about some human rights and come to recognise torture, infanticide, and human sacrifice as morally acceptable?

Meanwhile, there seems to be considerable disagreement about what is acceptable practice right now. Whenever I open a newspaper, columnists seem to be arguing about moral issues. Can doctors assist people who say they want to die, or induce abortion in the second trimester of pregnancy? Is there anything wrong with creating animals with human genes, and are quotas for disadvantaged groups fair or unfair? On a personal level, there is the same controversy and confusion. My vegetarian friends disapprove of my carnivorous habits, while I think they are being sanctimonious. We argue over whether one-night stands are fun or hurtful, whether smoking and heroin addiction are just personal choices or morally irresponsible. Some of the moral beliefs I held in the past have changed over the years. I used to be indifferent to charity appeals, now I think I should contribute some money. I have become more tolerant about some matters, less about others.

I am aware that I and most other people have visceral responses to the behaviour of others. I sometimes feel scorn, disgust, horror, admiration, and approval when witnessing or reading or hearing about others' behaviour. Such reactions may be accompanied by confident verbal declarations such as 'That was an utterly heartless thing to do' or 'It was absolutely right of her to resign under the circumstances' or 'He is fundamentally untrustworthy and should be shunned.' Such utterances are considered to express 'moral judgements'; they are ubiquitous in conversation and appear in editorial writing. Sometimes they are said to express people's 'moral convictions.' But I have to wonder whether people who say and write such things are doing more than venting their feelings. Are they actually making claims that could be true or false about the actions, events, situations, and persons they seem to be commenting on? And, if so, are they ever fully justified in making such claims? Indeed, I am led to wonder about moral knowledge— whether there is any such thing, and if so, what is involved in having more or less of it.

Does anyone actually know that it is 'morally good' to risk one's life to save a baby from a burning building and 'morally wrong' to leave a baby alone and unfed? Or are we just in the habit of applauding the former and feeling shocked by the latter? And what about those people in history? Did they think they knew that it was right and proper to flog their exhausted carthorses, though they were in fact mistaken about this and it was neither right nor proper? Is there a set of moral truths or moral facts that is partly known by some people but fully understood by no one? If so, how it is possible to get to know more of them? And what would be the point of acquiring more moral knowledge anyway? Is it so important just to 'be right'?

I feel strongly that the current treatment of prisoners is morally indefensible and that assisted suicide is justifiable if the person asking for it is in intractable pain, or facing that prospect, or if no one has ever emerged from his or her present condition to go on to live a pleasant life. I am reluctant, though, to say that I 'know' these things. Perhaps I should say that I 'conjecture' that the treatment of prisoners is morally indefensible? But this seems to imply that there is a fact of the matter and that someday I may come to know whether I am right. Really, all I am confident of is that I feel strongly about certain things, weakly about others, and I notice that others feel the same or differently about them.

The variety and changeableness of moral opinions, then, leads me to doubt that I really know anything about what is morally right, wrong, permissible, forbidden, and obligatory–or indeed what this term 'moral' really applies to. It also leads me to doubt that anyone else knows better than I do. People argue about these subjects, but I find myself sceptical about whether we can get to the moral truth by discussing and debating. In the arguments I have with people about moral subjects, we seem to be giving reasons that explain our feelings about things. Sometimes these feelings change as a result of what was said in the discussion, but discussing and arguing don't seem to me much like proving or demonstrating as they are done in mathematics or like amassing evidence from historical records or like performing and interpreting scientific experiments.

I can appreciate at the same time that the fact that other people believe things that I do not and do not believe things that I do, or that they have different feelings and dispositions from mine, does not imply that everyone is at sea when it comes to moral matters and that no one's convictions are better than anyone else's. The fact that people believe different things and are not always persuaded by moral arguments might be no more surprising than the fact that few people can follow mathematical proofs beyond some elementary level or understand a scientific paper or medical article establishing some important conclusion. There may be actual proofs of moral claims in the theoretical literature that have not filtered down to me.

Moreover, despite my sense that moral arguments don't really establish the truth or falsity of moral judgements in a knock-down way, some judgements strike me as better supported by arguments and considerations, whereas others seem to express mere prejudices or superstitions, akin to other non-moral prejudices and superstitions. On matters of health — what is good for the body — I know that many people are misinformed, believing for example that eggs and butter are dangerous to them, that getting their feet wet can bring on a cold, and that everyone needs to drink two litres of water a day. I know these beliefs to be poorly supported by the evidence. Many people are misinformed as well about such matters as climate change or the effects of punishment. For example, many people doubtless believe that the threat of capital punishment deters would-be murderers, although evidence for this claim is lacking. Perhaps some changes in moral opinion, in individuals, or in entire societies are definitely changes for the better, replacing moral error with moral knowledge.

Yet the observation that people can be misinformed about health matters, the planet, or how society works gives me a second reason, besides the sheer variety of opinions held by intelligent people past and present, for being uncertain as to whether there can be moral knowledge. Where convictions about nutrition or the efficacy of punishment are concerned, there are methods of getting to the truth. Experiment, observation, and analysis of the data can eventually determine what is the case. Either eggs are conducive to heart attacks, given the existence of certain preconditions, or they are not; either global warming is principally man-made or it is not, and we will eventually know which, or at least some particular opinions on these matters will come to seem outlandish. I do not see, however, how we could make experiments or observations to establish whether capital punishment was right or wrong. Moral convictions do not seem to be causal beliefs about what happens if, or whenever, something else is done or occurs, or about the powers of certain substances like eggs, butter, and pomegranate juice. If I believe that capital punishment is wrong, I don't think that its 'wrongness' can be detected by meters or test-sticks or by the effects of the wrongness on the human organism.

But perhaps I am being overhasty in supposing that experiment and observation, combined with analysis, cannot enable us to decide who is right in any moral dispute and that experiment and observation will never be able to do so. After all, it took physics and chemistry thousands of years to get off the ground. Perhaps we have slowly been developing methods for distinguishing moral truth from error, or perhaps we are just on the verge of developing them. Alternatively, perhaps no complex methodology is needed. There may be people who are gifted with a particular kind of moral sensitivity and insight that enables them directly to perceive the moral qualities of actions, such as their acceptability or their wrongness, in the same way that I directly perceive the blue colour of the sky. Then all we would need was a method for discovering who these oracular beings amongst us were. However, I see no way of identifying these experts, especially since those who make a profession out of speaking and writing about morality tend to disagree with one another.

At this point, a third reason for doubting that I have any moral knowledge, besides the variety of opinions and the absence of any agreed upon experimental method for deciding between them, occurs to me.

I can imagine various ways in which my individual existence within human society could have come about. A supernatural Being, the Creator of Heaven and Earth, may have fashioned me or my first ancestors in Its image and equipped me with the limbs, organs, and physiology that would enable me to survive at least for a time and to perpetuate my kind. Perhaps this Being has also equipped me with a mind that was stocked with or able to acquire various beliefs about better and worse situations and so to look to its own self-interest. It is possible that this Being has laid down and revealed moral commandments that correspond to Its preferences about how I ought to behave and that my intuitions about moral right and wrong have also been instilled in me by this supernatural Creator.

However, this supposition about the origins of my moral feelings and impulses raises many questions. Why should a supernatural Being have both the power and the desire to do exactly this? Why create a vast universe of billions of solar systems and then, on one tiny planet, create human beings to judge, reward, and punish them? Perhaps filling the universe with living creatures expresses this Being's love of creative activity and Its desire for variety, while Its creation of only one Earth and only one set of humans expresses a special focus and interest? But if so, it must be admitted that Its tastes are peculiar. Why do all creatures have finite life spans and why is death either preceded by old age and decrepitude or expedited by painful illness and disastrous accidents? A Being powerful enough to create this vast variety of species is surely capable of making life healthy and of infinite duration. Perhaps the love of variety requires death, so as to make room for more different species and it amuses the Being to outfit each species with beliefs and desires conducive to its preservation only until it can be replaced with the next generation. Or perhaps this Being knows that every creature will sooner or later tire of experience and wish for death as for a long sleep? Another hypothesis[4] that would better explain this situation is that there are many supernatural beings, each creating, in different parts of the universe, what they can. The Creator of our world is amusing Itself as children do when playing with their dolls, sometimes tenderly and sometimes cruelly.

These hypotheses are possible, but I do not judge their probability to be high. For the great age of the earth, the evidence of multiple extinctions, and the similarity of humans and apes lead me to doubt that human beings were created from nothing and for some purpose fully understood only by a supernatural Being. I prefer to search for other explanations of how my species came into the world, explanations which can perhaps shed some light on how I know a few things about what I ought and ought not to do and what is good for me, and also on why I have the moral feelings and make the moral judgements that I do.

Here is another possibility. In the beginning, there were only particles and forces, or some unknown substrate of both that produced them. Some of the particles combined into atomic and molecular clumps under the influence of the laws of physics and chemistry. As crystals, though non-living, possess the power to draw materials out of solution that replicate their structure, I can imagine that such clumps and strings grew and that pieces broke off and grew into new clumps and strings. Some of these would have had slightly different shapes and physical and chemical properties to others, rendering them better able to grow and split off and so perpetuate their type. While many of these simple entities would have fallen apart or failed to grow or to split, each small difference that conferred stability and the ability to copy itself would have been found in greater numbers. By such a process I can imagine that, from crystals, simple forms of 'life' should have arisen—forms that took in nourishment, grew, reproduced themselves and, inevitably, worn down by the wear and tear on their bodies, ceased to function.

As time went on, these entities could have developed various tropisms—some moved towards the light, others moved away from it for safety. And eventually, over the more than four billion years we know the earth to have existed,[5] more complicated living things appeared which had appetites—they felt a sort of pleasure when satiated and an anxious, unpleasant sensation otherwise that motivated them to hunt or forage for food, or to graze, when their bodies needed nourishment. Those that did not feel uncomfortable and did not seek shelter when it was very cold or very hot perished. Those with certain desires and appetites for union with others reproduced their kind. In this way, I can imagine that nature has fashioned certain of my basic beliefs about what is good for me, and instilled in me certain desires and patterns of behaviour, without culture and education coming into it. I share certain dispositions with other mammals—such as the tendency to retreat from a very hot fire, to seek food when hungry, and to care for my young. No one needs to teach me that the blazing sun or the bitter cold and wind are uncomfortable—though as a child I was always being reminded to put on a coat—and that I should seek the shade or the warmth of a fire. No one needs to teach me that I need food, water, and rest. Indeed I must be cajoled and persuaded by others to brave the sun and wind when something makes this necessary, or to endure hunger, thirst, and tiredness for the purposes of culture.

Perhaps my basic moral feelings in response to occurrences I am involved in or observe are, like my other basic emotions, wired into me by nature. My primate ancestors have been found to punish antisocial behaviour in their fellows, and to react with gratitude and indignation to others who treat them in particular ways. These reactions are not true or false, they just are what they are and mine may be no different in that respect. Of course, I have received a more extensive education than apes and monkeys, thanks to the existence of language and cultural experimentation and learning taking place over more than ten thousand generations. But then perhaps my moral convictions and my tastes and preferences are only the results of my education as a person growing up in a Western European environment.

I have had something of a scientific and mathematical education. I have read certain novels and have been exposed to the opinions of parents, teachers and newspapers. I have been indoctrinated since childhood with other people's views about right and wrong, as well as their views about how the world works. I was punished for actions my elders frowned upon, and I was commended for behaviour of which my elders approved. The books I read and that were read to me planted in me the idea that children who behaved in certain ways were naughty and deserved punishment. Later, I heard sermons and read newspaper editorials and encountered moral philosophers who praised certain traits as good and noble. If I had had a different upbringing in some other part of the world, most of the contents of my mind, including my beliefs, convictions, tastes, and preferences, would be altogether different. Even my visceral reactions and my dispositions to act would undoubtedly be different. All I really seem to know is that other people in my culture are anxious for me to behave in certain ways and willing to back this up with praise or punishment.

Perhaps, then, the contents of my own mind and my reactions and dispositions are the products of my particular culture, as everyone else's are of theirs. Perhaps we simply go about in the world with different cultural and personal standards that overlap to some degree with other people's, but that are as different as the various national cuisines and formal dress styles. Perhaps we can articulate certain rationales for our standards, rationales that sound plausible to others in our culture or even subculture, but not necessarily to those outside it. The 'explanation' for why it is right to hang, disembowel, draw and quarter enemies of the regime convinced or would have convinced, had it been presented to them, my17th-century English ancestors, but it does not convince us, any more than the 'explanation' for why foot-binding as the correct practice for young girls convinces us.

However, the recognition that my beliefs, feelings, and attitudes have been formed by my parents, teachers, and reading materials still does not quite persuade me that there is no such thing as moral knowledge.

When I was young, and when the grown-ups of my culture told me what was the case in the world, or what was the right way to do something, or that I ought to do something, they were often—though not always—right. For example, they impressed on me that I had better get 81 when I multiplied 9 by 9; that when beating egg whites, I ought to stop when the peaks were stiff; and that I ought to understand the material if I wanted to pass a difficult test. They imparted knowledge—useful knowledge—to me in this fashion. Perhaps through long experience and practice, my elders were also able to accumulate moral knowledge, which they have passed on, along with some moral errors. So I do not see that the fact that I have acquired my beliefs through instruction by my elders and by reading their books implies that no one knows anything about morality. Their experience has given them knowledge of mathematics, cookery, etc. So why not morality too? While their understanding of these subjects may be fallible or incomplete, it seems absurd to maintain that no one knows how one ought to do a long division problem or put together and bake a soufflé, or how to operate a blowtorch safely. And if many of these how-to-do-its are known to experienced people, why should all other instructions about how to behave, the 'oughts' and 'must nevers' of morality, be unknown to everyone?

A fourth and final reason for scepticism now occurs to me. Perhaps, despite having acquired such moral knowledge from books and teachers, no one ever acts out of motives other than self-interest. If I help old ladies across the street, it is because I derive pleasure from doing so, or because I am pained by seeing them stumble. If I give money to charity organisations, it's because it relieves my unpleasant guilt about starving children. If tell the truth it's because I am a poor liar and fear the consequences of being found out in a lie. If I had the Ring of Gyges that, according to Plato, made its wearer invisible, I might be tempted to get up to all sorts of thieving behaviour that I now regard as too risky. If all my actions are performed out of self-interest, of what conceivable use would it be for me to 'know' that action A was morally wrong, or that person P was immoral? For if it was in my self-interest to do A or to associate with P, I would do it, regardless of whether it was 'moral' or not, and if it was not in my self-interest, I would desist from A and shun P. Knowing their moral properties would not influence my behaviour one jot. Perhaps there is a whole raft of moral truths, including some that various people know, but they make no difference to anything because no one is actually motivated to act by knowing them.

This strikes me as a very strong and compelling argument for doubt—not just about the truth of any moral claims, but about the very practices of moral discussion and debate that surround me. Perhaps I should simply ignore them and carry on living, seeking my own advantage and moderating my behaviour just enough to avoid retaliation from others in case seeking my own advantage proves disadvantageous to them.

Yet however tempting this position seems, something in me rebels against it. When someone deceives me, or deliberately sets out to harm my reputation, I feel anger and resentment, and sometimes a desire for revenge which seems to be justified by the fact that the other party *ought not* to have hurt me in the way they did. I am sure the offender felt they were getting something out of it, even if it was just sadistic pleasure rather than some material or competitive advantage. Harming me was in their self-interest—but it was not *right*! Conversely, it occurs to me that I could be angry and resentful about someone's behaviour when they had done nothing wrong, and that my punishing them in that case would be wrong on my part. So even if I often or even mostly act out of self-interest, deriving pleasure from actions deemed 'morally good,' and avoiding actions deemed 'morally bad' out of fear of punishment, it still seems possible that a reason or a motive for doing something could possibly be that it is the morally right thing to do.

As a result of these reflections, I can see no way of deciding whether my moral convictions and opinions bear any relationship to 'knowledge.' Some considerations speak for the possibility of moral knowledge, others against it. I think that to make any headway in this subject, to discover whether anything can be known about morality, I shall have to cast aside decisively all the moral beliefs that I have ever held and begin my reasonings from scratch. This is the only way I can now see to try to gain clarity about these confusing issues and to establish whether moral knowledge is possible, whether it would be worth having or make a difference, and if so why and how.

Putting aside all my moral beliefs and beliefs about morality will not be easy. I shall need to dispense with my most firmly held convictions about torture and slavery, as well as with my beliefs about how friends ought to behave towards one another. But I shall also need to cast aside all my suspicions about how morality is related to self-interest and adopt an agnostic stance on that question. I shall have to suppose as well that I do not have a clear idea of what morality is—what makes something a moral issue, rather than a question of etiquette or a question of practicality.

To clear the ground, I shall even doubt that what I am inclined to call 'moral convictions' or 'moral opinions' or 'moral judgements' actually are or express beliefs—beliefs like the conviction or judgement that it is raining, or the opinion that the sun will rise tomorrow. I shall suppose only that I experience certain feelings—including hope, fear, disgust, admiration, contempt, worry, foreboding, and joy—when I observe or contemplate actions, events, situations, and persons, and that these feelings sometimes prompt me to utter sentences of the type usually regarded as moral judgements.

That I have these feelings as I move around in the world is undeniable. I contemplate with a mixture of pleasure and foreboding the long drive I am about to undertake; with admiration, the graceful movements of skaters on the canal; with disgust, the mess at the bottom of my rubbish bin. I feel uplifted when I see the first leaves unfurling on the trees in the spring. I also feel shock and horror when I read about a particularly lurid murder and resentment when one of my superiors denies what I feel to be a perfectly reasonable request. But I shall have to persuade myself that although I see actions, situations, events, and persons—the usual targets of moral evaluation—as having evaluative qualities, as being 'good' or 'bad' in all kind of respects, and although I sometimes feel quite emotional about what goes on in the world, nothing that happens or that anyone does is really morally good or bad.

I shall suppose that all moral judgements reflect illusions of a certain sort, that none of the targets of evaluation really possess the qualities of the contemptible or admirable, right or wrong, permissible or impermissible or obligatory, that no actions are virtuous or vicious. I shall suppose that the moral valuing and disvaluing of particular targets that I experience are only subjective and personal reactions to the world, and that none of the moral beliefs and convictions in my mind reflects reality.

This total suspension of belief in moral knowledge is going to be difficult. How can I doubt that I hold beliefs about what is morally prohibited, that these beliefs represent something in the world, and that at least some of them are true? I find it hard to doubt that if I were to create a spectacle by dousing my kitten with gasoline and setting her alight, this would simply be wrong, and wrong regardless of what I or anyone else thinks or feels about it. It will be difficult for me to get into a properly sceptical frame of mind, ignoring what my emotions seem to tell me, and difficult to set aside all my deepest moral convictions about warfare, sexual and economic exploitation, and political corruption. But I can see no other way forward unless I can manage to clear the ground of all my confusions and find a proper starting point for enquiry.

Enquiry II

The Enquirer decides to doubt whether any actions, situations, events, and persons can be really good or bad, right or wrong, morally permissible or morally impermissible.

I seem to belong to a highly judgemental species, and it is hard to refrain from judging and evaluating, praising and blaming. All around me, people are rating, reviewing, giving stars, thumbs up and down to films, hotels, household appliances, and life events. They write restaurant reviews that say 'The fish was underdone and the staff were rude,' as though the fish and the staff actually had those qualities, and they expect others to make use of the 'information.' They gossip about one another's personal lives and decisions, admiring and disapproving of their friends' actions. Human beings slap fines on one another and cart others of their species off to jail. They also award them medals, badges, and diplomas for achievements deemed meritorious. I find myself constantly judging my food and drink for its tastiness and value for money. I cannot seem to help judging some kinds of people for what I take to be their moral qualities, as well as for their nonmoral qualities of being politically savvy or hilarious, or displaying athletic prowess or artistic ability.

To help me to determine whether there are any moral truths that I can come to know, I will try to adopt an objective, strictly value-free perspective on the world. I will suppose not only that nothing is morally right or morally wrong, but also that nothing is really beautiful or ugly, good or bad, worth pursuing or pointless. Further, I will suppose that when the world changes, or anything changes in the world, it is never better or worse than it was before.

Everything is what it is on my new assumption. The spotted toadstool and the warty toad are no uglier than the peacock or the racehorse; the worm is not inferior to the human species that has its Mozarts, Newtons,

                    http://dx.doi.org/10.11647/OBP.0087.02

and Lauren Bacalls. All cultural forms—laws, governments, styles of dress, conventions—are neither good nor bad; they too are as they are. They arise and perish as conditions change. Events that I used to consider as terrible disasters and moral horrors, such as the Holocaust or Napoleon's assault on Russia, are no worse or more unfortunate on my new supposition than ample harvests and peace treaties. Disease and death are no worse than health and recovery. There is nothing to celebrate or regret. It is simply a fact that things happen. I have my preferences, to be sure. I admire and deplore, I rejoice in certain events that I perceive as having personal importance, and I regard with deep dismay certain political events. I understand words like 'atrocity,' 'tragedy,' and 'benefit.' But when people rejoice over the birth of a child or some prize that comes their way, I shall not suppose that there is anything intrinsically good in this event, only that it is the sort of event that induces 'happy' words and gestures in people who are related to the event in a particular way.

It is difficult for me to keep this neutral picture in mind. It is hard for me not to consider the feathers of the peacock more beautiful than the warts on the toad, to refuse to admit that some people are genuinely annoying, and to deny that the maggots in the rubbish bin are really disgusting. I cannot help but judge some houses and flats nicer and better located than others. My habits of evaluation keep overwhelming me even while I try to keep them at bay. This knife is terrible! I think; it mashes the tomato I am trying to slice. This soup is delicious; the hint of basil makes it so. I have stipulated that evaluative properties and relations of better-and-worse do not exist, but I have difficulty *believing* the world to be value-free insofar as I do not experience it as such.[6]

I might however conceive the world as free of values by considering the following. All that really exists are the unperceivable atoms or subatomic particles and the forces described by physics that are the building blocks of the physical world, including everything from stars and planets to human beings and their brains. The world of animals, people, features of the landscape, and manufactured objects is simply an appearance conditioned by my brain. The 'scientific image' of a value-free world seems to lie 'behind' the image of nature carried about with me in my mind. At the subatomic level, science tries to account for matter, force, gravity, and also time and space. At the atomic level, it explains chemical reactions. At the level of physics and physiology, science tries to explain how molecules and physical and chemical processes generate all the various worlds of experience in all conscious creatures, including birds and mammals and perhaps fish and insects too. The sciences give me a representation of the world that is unaffected by people's neurological idiosyncrasies and cultural upbringing. A physicist can be colour-blind and tone deaf and still make discoveries. Physicists in Japan share a common scientific image of the fundamental particles and forces with physicists in Nigeria.

I am confident that there is no good or evil amongst the particles and forces that are the basis of everything that exists. Nothing they do is 'better' or 'worse' than anything else. So values are not to be found in the world as physics — or physics and chemistry — describes it. The same is true, I think, of the world as the biologist describes it. He or she may note that a certain gene confers resistance to a certain virus, while another gene predisposes one to malaria. It is 'good for' organisms to be resistant to viruses and 'bad for' them to catch malaria, but it is hard to see the world as better or worse off with one less or one more sick animal, except insofar as we care about the flourishing of the animal more than the flourishing of viruses and bacteria. I feel sorry for the young antelope caught in the jaws of the crocodile, but to the scientist this is just another event of the sort that sometimes happens: a crocodile is nourished, there is one young antelope less in the world, but this is neither fortunate nor unfortunate in itself. The growth of a cancer is a misfortune from the human point of view, but considered abstractly, it is just a physiological process that is what it is.

Now, however, it occurs to me to wonder why I should accept accounts of the world given by physics, chemistry, and biology as *true*, as constituting knowledge — indeed as being paradigmatic of what knowledge is.

I accept this image, I think, in part because I value the understanding, power, and enjoyment that it gives me. I perceive its body of descriptions as having an especially valuable property — the value of being useful. I see it as better than the common-sense account of the world, insofar as science permits us to predict what is going to happen, to advance our interests in light of our expectations, and to exercise control over nature and direct nature to ends we consider (mistakenly or not) to be good. At the same time, I may fear science — or fear its effects. The technological mastery of nature is not without terrible by-products: weapons, including weapons of mass destruction, pollution, and perhaps certain unpleasant psychological effects that arise from living in an advanced technological age. I also admire science as an institution, an institution with a track record, not only of technological products, but of self-refinement. As an enterprise, science is not only a way of learning about nature, but a way of learning how to learn about nature—through the development of instruments and methods, including experimental protocols and mathematical and statistical techniques. It can uproot and supplant harmful and idle superstition.

So the acceptance of the value-free scientific image of the world itself reflects a number of my values and my attitudes of approval and disapproval. This leads me to wonder whether the vocabulary of physics, chemistry, and biology is the only one in which we can express our knowledge of the facts. Surely there are 'unscientific facts'—matters of common sense and statements that are just as true as the statements of science. For example, I think I know that stoplights are red and that bread is nourishing to humans, though stoplights and bread do not belong to the ontology of physics and chemistry. And now the following idea occurs to me. Perhaps there are many types or levels of 'real things' described by various ontologies, or theories of what exists. One kind of reality is possessed by the subatomic particles that we will never be able to see or describe in sensory terms. Some of these entities do not even interact with us in a causal way—their existence is postulated on the basis of very good evidence. Our best science tells us they must exist and be the foundations of everything. In the middle of the range are the perceptible, stable, middle-sized objects we see, name, and interact with, such as animals, people, plants, stones, and bones. These do not exist for all possible sorts of perceivers—not for worms and fish— though they may exist for birds and apes. In any case, all humans recognise these as real entities. Socks and clocks are perhaps not quite as real; not all cultures can identify them, name them, or see 'what they are.' Socks and clocks are more dependent on, more relative to cultural practices, than are stones and bones, and far more dependent on and relative to cultural practices than subatomic particles and fundamental forces.

Even further away from the 'ultimate reality' of the subatomic level are the imperceptible things wholly dependent on human interests and practices,[7] such as 'the prevailing rate of interest,' which do exist, and postulated 'things' whose existence may be in doubt—such as the 'business cycle.' Belief in these 'social constructions' is surely causally potent— people make decisions and act on the basis of what they believe about the business cycle. But they also acted on the basis of their beliefs about witches in previous centuries. There is no causal potency ascribable to witches as opposed to belief in witches, and perhaps none to the business cycle either.

Another kind of reality is possessed by fleeting and intangible, but still intersubjectively perceptible things such as rainbows and reflections in still ponds. And yet another is possessed by entities that are fleeting, intangible, and private, such as dreams, fantasies, and afterimages. They really happen and may even possess causal powers—an afterimage might delight me, a dream might obsess me. Then there are fictional characters. Emma Bovary and Othello are really characters in a book and a play, though they do not exist in the same way that my next-door neighbours do. Thinking about them, or observing actors representing them, can have powerful effects— they may move me emotionally, or inspire me, or appal me.

I am willing to say not only that snow and plums exist, but also that I can *know* that snow is white and plums are purple, and that this is common knowledge. Agreement about such matters arises, I think, from a basic similarity in all human beings, perhaps because we all trace our ancestry back to a very small number of founders. Thus our sensory systems, our fears and our biological needs, are sufficiently alike for us to agree in many of our judgements. The exchanges between cultures of knowledge, technology, and material goods lead not to homogeneity, but to wide consensus and adoption of objects and practices. Socks and clocks, along with 'the prevailing rate of interest,' get to be known about and used by more and more people as time goes on.

The observation that the entities I take to be commonsensically 'real' vary from culture to culture and that the claims about them that I take to be commonsensically 'true' are those on which there is wide consensus in our culture gives me another opening into radical doubt about values. For precisely where there is insufficient similarity in people to support consensus on everyday judgements, I am apt to become doubtful whether the objects referred to really possess the properties I and others sometimes ascribe to them. For example, I hesitate to say that broccoli tastes good without adding the qualification 'to me.' The good taste of broccoli does not seem to reside in it in the same way as the whiteness of snow, which all normal perceivers agree it possesses. The wrongness of torture does not seem to reside in it in the same way as its painfulness, which all normal observers agree it possesses.

But what if every human being's experience when they ate broccoli was pleasurable, if there were as much agreement about broccoli's taste as there is about the colours of ripe tomatoes and snow? Would it be right to say that I and other human beings *know* that broccoli tastes good? If someone was born who, unlike everybody else in their world, did not like broccoli, would it not be reasonable to describe this person as 'taste blind' for the good taste of broccoli, on analogy with colour-blindness. If broccoli were the main nutritional staple in the human diet, I think we might have to describe the mutant as 'taste-blind' and as deficient in that regard. Indeed, we seem to think of young children that they ought to be taught to like things they don't spontaneously like—including broccoli. This suggests that there really is some kind of value inherent in broccoli.

Yet I resist saying that everyone else in the imaginary society, apart from the mutant, *knows* that broccoli tastes good in exactly the same way that most people in our society know that ripe tomatoes are red. I think that this is because in my own world, I am aware of widespread disagreement about the good taste of broccoli. A substantial number of people do not like broccoli. I don't judge them to be 'taste blind' because liking broccoli is not a very important asset for getting along in our society. Only in certain subcultures do we try to get our children to like it—elsewhere it does not matter whether they like it or not. Really, I am inclined to think, broccoli isn't delicious or not delicious—some like it, some don't. And I am beginning to suspect that moral qualities are matters of taste as well.

When I first began to assemble reasons for doubting that I could have any moral knowledge, I considered the possibility that my basic beliefs and reactions were wired into me by evolution or society. This suggested to me that they could not be true—they were just the beliefs and reactions I happened to have. Let me now venture a hypothesis about why I might experience the world as loaded with evaluative properties and relations when it is not. The hypothesis is that my habits of evaluation, and so all my evaluative beliefs, and all the evaluative properties and relations I seem to perceive in natural and artificial things and in people and situations arise in me as a result of my personal Neurological Constitution and my society's Cultural Transmission. These two forces, I suppose, cause me to form beliefs about right and wrong and to ascribe evaluative properties to various objects of moral appraisal that they do not have. They induce me to believe, for example, that the world became morally better when women earned the right to vote in some countries, and that genocide is morally abhorrent. Both my own Neurological Constitution and my society's Cultural Transmission are able to induce in me illusions of moral properties and relations and the misapprehension that moral entities like 'vice' and 'justice' actually exist and can be described.

Why should I accept the hypothesis that my Neurological Constitution and my society's Cultural Transmission deceive me in this fashion?

I reflect first that how an animal (and I have no doubt that I am a member of a particular animal species) perceives the world depends on its sensory system. Evolution has given me a brain of a certain sort, hardwired in certain ways typical of my species, though it is also responsive to teaching and able to learn from experience and observation. My experiences arise from the interaction between light waves and my visual system, between sound waves and my auditory system, between chemicals and my olfactory system and taste buds, and from interactions between my skin and limbs and the forces responsible for the solidity of conglomerates of atoms and that move things around. Things that are colourless in themselves—waves or particles of light, atoms, molecules arranged in certain patterns—somehow interact so that some conscious creatures including myself see the world as composed of coloured objects. Different species of animals have different optical systems that make different colours or no colours appear to them—pigeons, for example, and other birds, are sensitive to portions of the electromagnetic spectrum that are invisible to humans and can see colours that we cannot. Humans themselves vary in the colours they can see. Many men are colour blind, and many women have enhanced colour vision.

A world in which there were no perceivers—neither animal nor human—would not be a colourful world because no particular colour would be assignable to any object. In such a world, there would only be dispositions on the part of objects to produce diverse colour experiences in differently endowed sensitive beings. Further, no two of us are exactly alike. The sizes and shapes of our limbs and organs, the various textures of our hair and colours of our eyes, make each of us a little different from all the rest. Although we physically resemble, for the most part, the people amongst whom we live, each of us is physically and psychologically a unique individual. Within the normal or typical range, two people can perceive the world differently, without either one representing the world correctly. So although there is a characteristically human way of seeing colours, shapes, and distances, within the typical, normal range we may each see and experience the world a little differently. Whose particular, unique way of seeing red and applying the term 'red' to objects in our common world is 'right' in that case? And why should I suppose that one person's way of 'seeing' torture is right and another person's is wrong?

The second force I suppose responsible for how I see the world is Cultural Transmission. The personality and character as well as the physical features of each person arise not only from their genetic make-up, but from their environment and its role in their development, from the things individuals do to themselves or that others have done to them, such as overeating or forcing them to play sports. So the living individual is a product of heredity, development, socialization, and self-fashioning.

Like everyone else, I have what I shall call a Normative Kit, a unique collection of beliefs—or whatever is expressed by my evaluative thoughts and judgements about actions, events, situations, and persons—along with dispositions to respond emotionally to them, and behavioural tendencies with respect to them. This Normative Kit has arisen through the interaction of Nature and Culture. This is simply a fact about me—a neutral, nonevaluative fact. The contents of my Normative Kit can be described in purely factual terms, though the contents are themselves values. My personal Normative Kit consists of a set of *preferences* (for example: I don't like my scrambled eggs to be too runny); a set of *emotional reactions* to the thought of certain ways of doing things, or perceiving them being done (for example: I feel contempt at the thought of anyone's cheating on their exams); and a set of *tendencies to respond* to certain pleasing or displeasing happenings and doings (for example: I usually like people who show that they like me). My Normative Kit, I shall suppose, is whatever it is and has only partial overlap with anyone else's, insofar as it is conditioned by my unique Neurological Constitution and the particular Cultural Transmission to which I have been subjected.

Reminding myself of the role of my unique Neurological Constitution in determining my unique Normative Kit helps me to keep the hypothesis of a value-free world before my mind. The colours of things are not really in them—rather, they come into being when a particular Neurological Constitution encounters a visible object, and there are as many differently coloured worlds as there are observers. In the same way, the goodness and betterness of my targets of moral appraisal, I now suppose, are not really in them either. They too come into being when a particular Neurological Constitution encounters an action, event, situation, or person of a particular sort. As it is misleading to ask what the real colour of a thing is, independent of any observer, it is misleading to ask what the real moral quality of any such target is.

By reflecting on Cultural Transmission, I can reinforce this impression. As individuals differ from one another within a culture, so cultures differ from one another, each seeing the world and valuing things in somewhat different ways and each inculcating those values in its members. My culture has given me myths and stories about good and evil, right and wrong, and lectures about the permissible, the forbidden and the obligatory. The novels I have read, the films I have seen, the friends and relatives from whom I have sought advice, and with whom I have discussed and gossiped — all of these sources, together with the newspaper articles and editorials, and historical, sociological, anthropological, and philosophical books have shaped the contents of my Normative Kit. Relatives, friends, and other authorities have punished me for what they called my 'bad' deeds and praised me for what they called my 'good' deeds.[8] The way I react to insults and oversights, or acts of kindness is conditioned by Cultural Transmission. So are my dispositions to act — to help others or to ignore them. As a result, my beliefs and practices are typical of educated Western Europeans of my age group and family background, and untypical of other populations. The Normative Kits of South Sea Islanders and the Inuit are accordingly different from mine, but mine is also different from my next-door neighbour's.

So I am persuaded that my Neurological Constitution and the Cultural Transmission I have been subjected to explain my Normative Kit. They determine fully whether I see boxing as a shocking display of brutality or as a fun spectator sport, and whether I favour abortion or see it as baby-murder. This is not to say that my Normative Kit is fixed for all time. It changes in response to new experiences and developments in the surrounding culture. But reflection on the sources of my Normative Kit is beginning to persuade me that the moral qualities I am in the habit of ascribing to actions, events, situations, and persons and that I suppose I perceive in them could not really belong to them. I am on pretty firm ground in supposing that it is just true that coal is black and that water is liquid, even if these judgements depend on my having the sensory system I do, but only because I share the basic elements of my sensory system with almost everyone else in the world, no matter where they live and what their culture is like. But I manifestly do not share a moral appraisal system with almost everyone else in the world. And if evaluative properties are observer-dependent, and if observers vary a great deal, it is hard to see how one culture or one individual could come to see things as they really are, morally speaking, in the same way I see coal as black and water as liquid.

On the suppositions about my Normative Kit that I have just made, how should I now understand moral discourse — the voicing of moral judgements, disagreements, disputations, and reconciliations carried on live or in print? Is nobody actually 'right' or actually 'wrong'? What is going on when people engage in moral argument and pronounce moral judgements if they are not describing the world, or at least attempting to describe the world, as it really is?

I can think of the human world as a collection of people who interact with one another linguistically, socially, and politically. Their minds, like mine, are stocked with ideas, attitudes, and emotions, which sometimes lead them to speak or write declarative sentences such as 'Abortion is wrong,' 'Abortion is murder of the innocent,' 'Abortion ought to be prohibited by the state,' or to issue imperatives such as 'Ban abortion now!' Others have in their Normative Kits the ideas expressed by sentences like 'Abortion is every woman's right' and 'A foetus is not a person with a right to life,' and they are inclined to utter imperatives like 'Hands off legal abortion!' Perhaps they are, in effect, holding up placards or posting signs with these slogans written on them, and, as at a rally, they feel emotional about their cause and aim to change other people's minds and behaviour. I need not suppose that their placards convey information or are susceptible of truth or falsity.

To be sure, posted signs like 'Thin Ice' and 'Beware the Dog' give information as to what is the case. If I read these signs, I may come to believe, correctly, that the ice is thin and that there is a savage dog on the premises. But for the signs to have their intended effect of deterring people, it is not necessary for the ice to be thin and a savage dog to be present.

A sign held up by someone on a placard or posted on a piece of property is normally intended to move others to some kind of action. Behind these warnings and commands, I now realise, lie the preferences of the sign-posters. Someone who posts the 'Thin Ice' warning wishes for people not to try the ice, and someone who posts the 'Beware the Dog' sign wants them to stay off their property. These signs function as a warning about what could happen if a person proceeds further. What could happen if the command is disobeyed or unheeded may be left to the imagination — which can conjure up for itself the spectacle of falling through the ice or being mauled. It is assumed by the sign-poster that the people who read these notices will prefer staying dry to trying to walk on the ice and remaining unbitten to venturing onto the property. When people ignore such signs it is because they want to go further, crossing the lake or robbing a house. They may think either that the sign maker has exaggerated the risk or that the potential reward negates the risk.

It seems to me that something similar could be going on when people utter or write the declarative anti-abortion sentences above. The vocalisations and statements express the desires of the speakers and writers who have a preference for abortions not happening or, alternatively, for their happening sometimes. They are also warnings to others. Something unspecified but bad will happen, the signs imply, if abortion is permitted (or banned). But where 'Thin Ice' or 'Beware the Dog' will deter all but a few hardy souls from proceeding further, the people who sport anti-abortion signs do not expect their signs to have this effect, though they hope, perhaps fervently, that they will. They likely believe that they are warning others of certain risks—the danger of moral harm—but they know that some who read their signs will either deny that there is any risk at all or will insist that the risk is worth taking.

Thus a defender of abortion might say: 'Yes, I see that proceeding further with the practice of legalising abortion is risky. Harm might indeed be done. But we must save women from death in backroom alleys, and we must try to ensure that children are loved and wanted. Their placards will read 'No interference with women's lives!' Their signs too convey a warning. They believe there is a risk of harm to women and children if the anti-abortion faction persuades too many people and succeeds in changing the law. They too want to warn that there is 'thin ice here.' Their opponents, the anti-abortion group, believe either that the risks to women and children are negligible, or that they can be minimised, or that the risks of moral harm to foetuses or even to society at large are more serious.

Accordingly, I suppose that people who utter the words 'Abortion is wrong' or 'Property is theft' desire that people neither perform nor undergo abortion or that people own no property. They also desire that their audiences adopt the same desires, the same view of the risks, and that they will in turn relay their preferences and risk assessments to others and attempt to prevent these performances, undergoings, and ownings. Our species argues and criticises, remonstrates and praises; we try to alter the Normative Kits of others and to defend or perhaps to improve our own. When I deliberate about whether some proposed course of action is right or wrong, I seem to hold up one sign at one moment, and another at another moment, and argue as though I were two people, with one or the other eventually dominating.

For centuries, I suppose, people have held up their placards and argued about them. The placards and the reasons people give for holding them up, or for being prepared to hold them up in discussion or debate, have effects on those who read them. They can change people's emotional reactions to actions, events, situations, and persons, or result in new forms of legislation and punishment, or in the repeal of laws and the abandonment of punishment. There used to be more 'Slavery is just' placards around than there are today. This can be explained by the interaction between the world and our Neurological Constitutions and the effectiveness of Cultural Transmission.

Yet something prevents me from thinking that this could be all there is to say about moral language and moral ideas. I am dismayed to read some of the placards people in my society hold up, declaiming on the radio and on television talk shows, snarling their opinions in the 'Comments' section of the newspaper. Many of these people seem wrong and misguided in their ideas and emotions. I think that people thoroughly disgusted by the thought of two men having sexual intercourse, or a mother nursing a baby in public, or an interracial couple holding hands ought to react differently. Conversely, they ought to respond more disgustedly, I think, to images of combat helicopters gunning down villagers. Yet, I can often understand what it must be like to have those feelings of disgust and enthusiasm for their moral causes, and why others are motivated to hold up those placards. If by contrast, someone professed to feel joy whenever he spotted a picture hanging crookedly on his wall and disgusted whenever someone plucked an apple from a tree and ate it, I would not understand this at all. So I seem to experience 'evaluative impressions,' as I shall call them, both about actions, situations, events, and persons, and also about other people's evaluative impressions of their targets of evaluation.

But maintaining my sceptical frame of mind, I shall continue to suppose that, regardless of anyone's outrage or dissatisfaction, the distribution of feelings, opinions, and practices that now exists in the world is no better or worse in any objective respect than the distribution of a generation ago or a thousand years ago. It was what it was, is what it is, and in the future it will be whatever it will be. As populations have grown taller since the middle ages through their interaction with the environment, I shall suppose that the beliefs, attitudes, and preferences in their heads have changed through their interactions and experiences, but I shall also suppose that there is no basis for saying that there has been any improvement or deterioration in their Normative Kits. I shall continue to suppose that my own feelings and preferences have no special weight. Mine are mine and other people's are theirs and no one's are better or worse, more enlightened or more benighted.

My current hypothesis is that all values in a value-free universe are the product of my own mind, as determined by my constitution and my culture. I am supposing that there can be scientific and common-sense knowledge about the properties things actually possess or once possessed — knowledge about plants, animals, stars, human thought processes, human societies, history and prehistory, and even knowledge about what various people's aesthetic and moral beliefs are, and how they were formed. But on my current hypothesis, there can be no moral knowledge, in the sense of knowing what one ought to do or what actions are morally impermissible or morally dubious. There are no moral truths that anyone knows, or could come to know.

Enquiry III

The Enquirer continues to ponder the notion of a value-free universe. She comes to the realisation that the world seems to be saturated experientially and linguistically with values. She entertains the possibility that a race of Destroyers of Illusion who use language differently has discovered that values are unreal and that there are only likings and dislikings. She discovers nevertheless that she does know at least one fact about what is good.

My working hypothesis is that I inhabit a value-free universe in which different people perceive different moral qualities in actions, events, situations, and persons in the same way that they perceive or do not perceive a good taste in broccoli. The world as I now see it contains an enormous variety of objects, living and non-living, as well as animals and people. They possess many qualities that can be discovered and described, but there is nothing actually right or wrong in this world and there are no obligations. No actions are demonic or saintly, cowardly or heroic, for to describe actions in this way is to imply that they are bad or good, wrong or right. There is absolutely nothing that we are morally obliged to do or to refrain from doing. It is as absurd to say 'Everything is morally permitted' as it is to say 'Some actions are not morally permitted.' Nothing is either permitted or not permitted.

It now occurs to me that there are two entirely different ways in which I might try to understand and apply the proposition that the universe is value-free. I could understand it to mean that it is philosophically correct to take a detached perspective on the struggles of a young faun in the jaws of a lion, or on the growth of a cancer in someone's body, or on torture or abortion. I could understand the proposal to imply that is appropriate to regard these events and situations as happenings in the world that just are, without seeing them as 'bad,' and that I should suspend my normal emotional reactions, my judgemental impulses. But if the world is really

    http://dx.doi.org/10.11647/OBP.0087.03

value-free, then it cannot be 'philosophically correct' or 'appropriate' to regard it in one way rather than in another. Whatever way I regard it— judgementally or nonjudgementally—is just the way I happen to regard it.

There is another way, however, to understand the proposal that the universe is value-free that is perhaps freer of implied prescriptivity. Let me try to imagine a world that is like our world in every way except that the people in it, having realised that there are no moral facts and no moral knowledge, never make moral judgements, and never tell others what they ought to do or are allowed to do. They never assert statements like 'You ought not to tell lies to your mother' or 'You should make occasional donations to charity.' They do, however, express their preferences, hopes, and fears. For example, a person belonging to this alien linguistic species might say 'I hate it when you lie to your mother!' or 'I wish more people would make donations to UNICEF!' These latter statements are genuine claims. They are true or false depending on whether the person who utters the words in quotation marks really has the emotions or wishes they report themselves as having.

These aliens, I shall suppose, see things as they really are and only as they really are. While they occasionally make mistakes, their mistakes are factual ones about properties and relations that could be instantiated in the world but that are not. They are not under the illusion that their objects of moral appraisal can actually possess such properties as being right or wrong, morally permitted or forbidden, morally courageous or morally cowardly. Indeed, they deny that objects and living beings can possess any features of goodness or badness, appropriateness or inappropriateness, suitability or unsuitability for purpose, normality (as opposed to averageness) or abnormality.

I shall call these people the Destroyers of Evaluative Illusion, or the Destroyers for short. They maintain that most of us live in a world of illusion, *projecting* our likings, dislikings, and preferences onto the world, that we 'see' our targets of appraisal as possessing evaluative properties that they do not possess. The language of the Destroyers, I might further suppose, contains no evaluative terms, only descriptive terms. They employ the term 'red' but not the term 'good.' They may describe a person as 'weighing 150 lbs,' but not as 'malicious.' And it seems to me that I can readily classify terms according to whether the language of the Destroyers could contain them (or equivalents for them) or not. For example:

Found in the Destroyers' Language	Not Found in the Destroyers' Language
DESCRIPTIVE	EVALUATIVE
dark	despicable
damp	disgusting
deciduous	duplicitous

On my current hypothesis, the Destroyers can *know* a room to be dark, a watercourse to be damp, a tree to be deciduous, a fence to be damaged, and a theorem to be demonstrable in classical mathematics, and they can assert in language that these things are so. But, lacking an evaluative vocabulary, they cannot say that an action is 'despicable,' or a policy decision 'disgusting,' or that a person is 'duplicitous.' To 'describe' actions, policies, and persons in this way is to imply that they ought to be some other way, and this is, in their view, an illusion that their purified language does not support.

But now, I have to wonder whether my notion of a suitably purified language really makes sense. Can I actually classify terms as descriptive and evaluative? Are there really two exclusive, non-overlapping categories here? 'Deciduous' seems to be a purely descriptive term, drawn from the science of botany with its technical language, but many everyday terms seem to be descriptive but at the same time evaluatively 'loaded.' On reflection, 'damp' is a term that usually has somewhat negative evaluative connotations. Damp towels and damp ceilings are usually 'worse' than dry ones. But garden soil could perhaps be 'nice and damp' where seeds have been planted. To describe a room as 'dark' is usually to imply that it is worse than a lighter room—and perhaps to imply that one ought not to buy a house with such a dark room; whereas to describe a film as 'dark' is often to imply that it is a good film, one that ought to be seen. And where do terms like 'zesty' and 'languorous' belong in the descriptive-evaluative scheme? Zesty is pungent-tasting, but in a good way, and languorous is slow, in a good way. Do the Destroyers avoid using these terms? Do they never describe a citrus drink as 'zesty' or a movement as 'languorous?'

Thinking further along these lines, I realise that many ordinary nouns, as well as ordinary adjectives, have evaluative connotations or can only be explicated with the help of words like 'good,' 'wrong,' 'ought to,' 'must,' or 'mustn't.' Take the words 'criminal' and 'film star.' To say of a person that she is a criminal is to imply (rightly or wrongly!) that she is a wrongdoer, doing things that she ought not to do, and perhaps to imply also that she ought to be punished or rehabilitated, rather than let go scot-free or ignored. To say of a person that she is a film star is to imply that she has admirable qualities, such as beauty and acting talent, that are deserved or possibly undeserved. 'Talent,' I ordinarily suppose, is both good to have and good to observe in action.

Implications of 'good' and 'bad' seem to permeate statements that at first glance are purely descriptive. Take, for example, the statement 'X beat up Y.' It is a bare statement of fact, one might think, not an evaluation. Yet it implies that X did something to Y that was bad for Y, though perhaps good for the victims Y had been bullying. Even the statement 'X gave £5 to Y' seems to have evaluative connotations; something good or bad was done here. My first impulse on hearing or reading this statement is to think that X did something good for Y. For I know that money is useful and that gifts of money or the repayment of loans are often appreciated. But on reflection I can see that it is possible that giving Y £5 might have been bad for them, if Y was expecting or hoping for more. Or X might have been the victim of a hold-up. The event of giving described could not have been 'neutral,' even if the statement does not logically imply either that something good was done for X or for Y or that something bad was done.

Does the value-free world of the Destroyers, which I suppose to be exactly like our world, except linguistically, contain 'criminals'? Surely it must contain people who stab others on lonely streets with knives and take their wallets, or who get into their houses when they are not home and make off with things. Do the Destroyers see nothing wrong with this? Do they not mind damp towels or value water for its excellent thirst-quenching properties?

On reflection, I can see that these absurd conclusions need not follow. Perhaps the Destroyers, rather than speaking a purified language, simply use and understand my usual vocabulary in a way consistent with the hypothesis of a value-free world. When one of the Destroyers says 'This towel is damp,' she is understood by the others to mean: 'This towel is slightly wet *and* I do not much like it this way *and* I predict that others wouldn't like it this way either.' When another of them describes a new drink as 'zesty,' he means: 'This new drink is mildly acidic *and* I like it *and* I would like it if you *and* other people liked it too.' As I imagine them, the Destroyers know that criminality is not 'wrong'—because nothing is really wrong—but they know that they and others do not like it when they are the ones stabbed or whose possessions are removed. So when one of them uses the word 'criminal,' they mean 'a person who does certain things I do not like done to me and that others do not like having done to them.' The term 'film star' in their language means something like 'a person who acts on screen in a way that many people like.' The Destroyers can even understand terms like 'election' in a roundabout way. Where we naively think of an election as a choice of the person believed to be the best–suited for some occupation or task, these people know that no one can really possess the property of being 'best-suited' for anything. To them, an 'election' is the choice of some person who is most liked when imagined in a specified occupation or task. 'Smith won the election for party leadership' for them means 'Smith was determined to be the person most liked by the electoral body when imagined in the role of party leader.'

The Destroyers, it seems, can think and say everything we can think and say. There is a translation for everything from our language to theirs. For example:

'Tigers are ferocious' » 'Tigers do things with their teeth and claws to other animals that the other animals do not like and that I and other people sometimes don't like either.'

'Bone is resilient' » 'Bone has a springy quality that I and others like'

'Water quenches thirst' » 'Water changes the condition of a thirsty person from one he doesn't like to one he likes better.'

'X morally wronged Y' » 'X did something to Y that I don't like and I would like it if others didn't like it either.'

The Destroyers consistently understand such claims by reference to their preferences and those of other living creatures rather than in terms of properties actually possessed by actions, events, situations, and persons. When the Destroyers describe tigers as 'ferocious,' they are under no illusion that the behaviour of tigers has the property of being 'bad' for their prey in the same way that their coats have the property of being striped.

But when a child discovers that tigers are ferocious or a medical student discovers that bone is resilient, it doesn't seem to involve a discovery about likings. No introspection, no consulting of their feelings, is involved. Rather, the child finds these things out by observing tigers in the wild or reading about their behaviour, and the medical student finds them out by studying bone and perhaps subjecting it to certain tests. And when I wonder whether a course of action is 'morally acceptable,' I am not wondering whether I like it or not. Suppose a factory owner 'likes' to imprison or shelter his workers at their sewing machines behind a barbed-wire fence for 12-hour workdays; the workers don't like it, and I don't like his liking it. It seems that I can *investigate* the claim 'The factory owner's arrangements are morally unacceptable,' whereas I don't need to investigate the claim 'I don't like the arrangements the factory owner likes that the workers don't like.' My wondering concerns whether I and others *ought* not to like the arrangements or *may* like them. But these 'oughts' and 'mays' have no meaning or application in a value-free universe.

I admit to being as confused as ever about the possibility of evaluative knowledge in light of these further reflections. On one hand, I think that the non-moral evaluative statements 'John knows that artichokes are delicious' and 'Marcia knows that cobras are dangerous' could be *true* if either sentence was uttered or written in a particular context. The first statement could be made by the parent of a child with sophisticated tastes; the second by the parent of a child who reads nature books. And if John knows that artichokes are delicious, and Marcia knows that cobras are dangerous, then the claims are true, at least in the context in which the relevant thoughts are had and the relevant sentences uttered. On the other hand, I don't see how John can *know* that artichokes are delicious, if there are cultures in which artichokes are spurned as inedible, or how Marcia can *know* that cobras are dangerous if there are cultures that keep a tame cobra around the house to eat rats. In these other contexts, Jack might be said to *know* that artichokes taste terrible and Miranda might be said to *know* that cobras are useful and friendly. It looks as though evaluative claims are 'true' or 'false' relative to particular cultures and that 'knowledge' depends on human likings, preferences, and circumstances.

Turning to moral properties and moral knowledge, I am equally torn. I am tempted to say that Mary can not only believe but *know* that the factory owner's arrangements are morally wrong. But factory owners and their social circle proceed as though they know that there is no problem with them, and many capitalists would deny that what Mary believes is correct.

Despite my ongoing uncertainty and confusion, I have now established a number of important things.

First, I recognise that my normal vocabulary for describing the world—the vocabulary I use when I am not thinking of it in physical and chemical terms—contains not only evaluative terms like 'good' and 'wrong,' but also nouns, verbs, adjectives, and adverbs that have evaluative connotations or implications when they appear in sentences that are used to make statements. The Destroyers have paraphrases for everything I say and write with this vocabulary, but I have not yet determined whether their paraphrases are really adequate—a problem I can defer until later.

Second, I no longer see a reason to suppose that beliefs that depend in some way on my Neurological Constitution and on Cultural Transmission are invariably false. My common-sense knowledge about the colour of snow, the temperament of tigers, and so on depends on both of these features, and I see no reason to deny that I know that snow is white and tigers are ferocious. Miranda, living in her culture of tame cobras, can know that they are useful and friendly, even if Marcia, living in her culture, knows that cobras are dangerous. At the same time, these observations do not help me to understand morality better, for morality does not seem to be simply a matter of common sense. And I am not entirely satisfied with the notion that Miranda, living in her culture, could know that torture is wrong, while Marcia, living in hers, could know that it is right.

At this point, turning my attention inwards, I find in myself—despite these worries—a certain conviction about what is good. The conviction is that my existence, at least for the time being, is better for me than my non-existence. Accordingly, the following statement, when uttered by me, is one in which I have complete confidence.

'My continued existence, at least right now, is good for me.'

I am also reasonably certain that anyone who is not in terrible emotional or physical pain can make the same judgement about their own existence.

Now, in uttering these words, or writing them, or merely thinking this statement, I have not deduced the fact that it is good for me now that I exist from the more general premise 'For everyone in the world, it is good for them now that they exist.' In fact I am sure this latter claim is false—there are people in the world suffering terrible torments who, at the moment, would be better off not existing and who wish they did not exist. But so what? I only judge that it is good *for me* that I exist *now*.

Nor am I asserting that my existence is in some absolute way a good thing. If someone were to insist that my continued existence is no better for the universe, that the universe is not a better place for my existing in it, I might have no argument against them. Maybe the world would be improved by my deletion from it. Nevertheless, I cannot doubt that *for me*, existence now is better than annihilation now.

Could I be wrong about this even if I am unable to doubt it?

The Destroyers will say that even if I know about myself that it is better for me to exist now, all that statement means is 'I like existing.' Or 'Right now, I'd rather exist than not.' Perhaps they are right. I will investigate this possibility later. Meanwhile, their paraphrase doesn't imply that I don't know that existing is better for me.

Doubtless both my Neurological Constitution and Cultural Transmission play a role in my conviction. An instinct for self-preservation seems to be a characteristic of all living things; few animals that did not take steps to prevent injury to themselves or death are to be found amongst my ancestors. All animals have some means of avoiding or defending themselves against threats and a built-in instinct to do so. And I am constantly warned about dangers to my existence by parents, friends, and authorities and given advice on how to avoid them. These warnings and urgings no doubt contribute to my sense that my life right this moment is valuable. Accordingly, my positive response to the thought of my continuing to exist and my negative response to the thought of my ceasing to exist arise from the interaction of my mind with a presentation to my consciousness in the form of a thought. But, as I have already established, all my thoughts seem to arise in this way and that does not prevent me from sometimes knowing what is the case at least where I am concerned.

Enquiry IV

The Enquirer discovers that, as far as her self-interest is concerned, there are certain things that are good and bad for her and therefore things she ought and ought not to do. The Enquirer discovers that she can also know something about what is in the self-interest of other people.

Very well. I seem to have discovered or realised that I know something about myself and what is good for me, what is in my own interest: namely, my present existence.

But this epistemic accomplishment is a long way from the discovery of any moral facts, facts about what is vicious or virtuous, morally permissible or impermissible, required or forbidden. It is unclear whether I know or can come to know any facts about what is good or bad, better or worse, besides this one. But it is a start, so I shall press onwards.

Reflecting further, I find in myself certain strong beliefs relating to my condition as an existing thing. These have to do with my biological needs as the living creature I know myself to be. My discomforts in particular are signs of danger—of threats to the existence that I currently prize. I know that I cannot survive for more than a few hours without special equipment in temperatures above 45°C or below 0°C, or without water for more than a few days, or without food for more than a month. Moreover, I doubt that I would survive for long if I were the last person left alive on earth.

But do I really *know* that it is better for me to be warm and dry, to be satiated rather than hungry, to be surrounded by other humans rather than alone? It seems that it is not always better for me to be in comfortable conditions. I may prefer to be cold and wet on an exciting rafting adventure that I would not have missed for anything, rather than warm and dry in my own sitting room; and my current state of hunger is not unpleasant since I know that I can look forward to the gratification of lunch soon. While it

                    http://dx.doi.org/10.11647/OBP.0087.04

would be a catastrophe if the rest of the human race were to vanish, leaving me in a world stocked with food and books, I like to be alone for some hours of the day. So my beliefs about what is good and bad for me do not generalise to all conditions. I think I can nevertheless claim to know that temperate conditions and sufficient food and water are generally better for me than extremes of temperature, starvation, and dehydration.

Recognising that these things are good and bad for me leads me to think that there are things I ought to do in order to secure companionship, food, water, and warmth and to avoid starvation, abandonment, and death. I ought to eat and drink from time to time, cultivate the attention of other human beings, and seek shelter when temperatures soar or plummet. Could I be under the illusion or misapprehension that I ought to do such things? I can imagine special circumstances obtaining under which it would be inadvisable to eat or drink or seek shelter or cultivate the attentions of people around me because of the dangers such activities posed. But I am not claiming that I ought always to do these things, given the opportunity. I am claiming only that for the sake of my own survival and welfare, I will mostly need to. (I know that birds fly, for example, even if there are a few exceptions, such as penguins.) I am confident accordingly that there are facts about what I ought to do.

Another fact I know about myself is that I probably have something of a future, and that my decisions and actions right now have a bearing on my future. I cannot be absolutely certain that I do have a future, for a sudden stroke could knock me out before I finish writing this sentence, or an asteroid colliding with earth could destroy me along with my environment next week. But I know is that the probability of my surviving for many years hence is very high.

The knowledge that I will likely survive for quite a long time into the future indicates to me that I ought to take it into account that some possible futures will be better or worse for me than others. Certain plans I formulate and act upon now will make my future security, opportunity, and happiness more or less than it would be had I formulated and acted upon other plans. While I am rarely certain of what is absolutely the best plan, or even whether, in some cases, I ought to be making a plan and carrying it out, rather than just waiting to see what happens, I am certain that some plans would be bad for me if I carried them out and that others are more promising.

Normally, I ought not to do anything that could threaten my immediate existence. I ought not to climb up a very rickety ladder to try to wire and hang a heavy chandelier, or to swim in shark-infested waters without special equipment if the opportunity immediately presents itself. Special circumstances might again make it necessary to do just what I ought not, in general, do, but it would be misleading to say that it is neither true nor false that swimming without equipment in shark-infested waters is a bad idea, and that there is no fact of the matter as to whether I ought to attempt DIY feats of the type just described.

The causes of my beliefs about what I ought to do and what to avoid doing lie in nurture as well as in nature. I have an innate fear of heights, thanks to my Neurological Constitution, and people informed me as a child of the dangers of electrical wiring. Movies and newspaper articles—Cultural Transmission—inspired my fear of sharks. Yet, their origins in nature and culture do not make these emotions irrational. And when the sentences below are uttered by me, in conditions in which the opportunities present themselves in a certain way, I am confident that they express my knowledge and understanding of the world and how things work or happen in it.

I ought not to try to hang this chandelier unassisted.

I ought not to go for a swim in these shark-infested waters.

There are many other 'ought' statements I could formulate that represent my knowledge of what it is good or bad for me to do right now, in these circumstances, whatever the circumstances may be at the moment. My knowledge of matters affecting my self-interest indeed appears to be extensive. Nevertheless, I anticipate two objections to my claim to know quite a bit about what's good and bad for me and what I ought to do.

First, someone might argue that it is not true that I ought not to perform various actions that are extremely risky and dangerous. For it might be the case that the universe would be better off without me, and, as long as this possibility cannot be ruled out, I cannot make the above claims with any confidence. Surely my going out of existence through electrocution or being eaten by a shark would be good for at least some others. Someone would get my job, and some others would enjoy my clothing and effects if my heirs donated them to be sold in a charity shop.

Perhaps there is a Supreme Being who oversees the Universe and who knows all that has happened in the past, is happening in the present, and will happen in the future, as well as all that might happen. Perhaps this Being knows that, were I to be annihilated, things would start to go better in the Universe. Very well, but I am not claiming to know that my existence is good for the Universe in the long run, only that it is good for me right now, and that since it is probable that I shall in fact continue to exist for some time, it is good for me to pursue and avoid certain things. From the mere possibility that, unbeknownst to me, the Universe would be better off without me, and that there is a God who knows this, it doesn't follow that I need not avoid doing foolish, self-destructive, or dangerous things. Perhaps my interest in existing and in preserving my existence and the good of the Universe are in conflict, but even if that is so, it does not defeat my claim to know what is in my own interest. I might, in a moment of psychological desperation and confused judgement, come to think that I would be better off not existing, but this thought could only occur to me in a state that I know at the moment that it would not be good for me to be in.

I can also appreciate that there are perspectives from which my existence does not matter, indeed, from which it does not matter how many or how few humans exist at all. I can imagine callous Martians, or callous foreigners, or even just people who dislike me intensely, holding the view that what happens to me—including my annihilation—does not matter one whit.[9] Nevertheless, this gives me no reason to take this position with regard to myself.

But now a second objection to my claim to know certain things about what I ought and ought not to do occurs to me. It is that I cannot see into the future with sufficient clarity to be certain that my continued existence will be better for me than my ceasing to exist at some moment hence. Perhaps I shall shortly be struck down with a dreadful illness involving prolonged suffering, or an invading army will capture me and subject me to lifelong solitary confinement punctuated by torture. If that happens, it might turn out to have been better for me had I electrocuted myself or been quickly consumed by sharks. Perhaps, unbeknownst to me, the disease has already taken hold, perhaps the invading army is quietly massing just up the road? In such cases, it will soon be the case that things would have gone better for me had I been destroyed. But, again, I do not see that the *possibility* that these things are, as I write, invisibly happening could imply that I cannot now know that I ought not to attempt this wiring task or go swimming in shark-infested waters. It is logically possible that by attempting to hang the chandelier I would release a pile of gold coins from the ceiling, whilst remaining unharmed. I can nevertheless deny that I ought to do this.

I do, however, have to admit that my ability to judge what will turn out to be best for me and so what I ought to do in various situations is hampered by my inability to foresee the future. When I move beyond the ubiquitous laws of physics that make severe electric shocks, falls from a great height, and attacks by certain predators invariably fatal and realise the multiplicity of causes and the role of chance, it seems that the full consequences of any decision I take are impossible to predict. Many occurrences make certain kinds of occurrence more likely in the future, but they do not necessitate them. A person who has already had one heart attack is more likely to have a second heart attack than a person who has had no heart attacks so far is to have a first one. Receiving a good education increases the likelihood of finding an enjoyable job. Having a sense of humour helps to attract a mate. But none of these further outcomes is guaranteed. All causes require the co-operation of other causes, and much happens by chance in the sense that from fortunate or unfortunate coincidences important effects can follow. I trip on a step and miss my usual bus; waiting for the next one, I meet a former colleague who offers me a new job. I win the lottery but have a miserable and vexed life trying to keep hold of my new-found wealth.

Yet I must make decisions about what will turn out to be good for me under conditions of uncertainty, and avoiding or postponing deciding is a way of deciding. So it is useful for me to establish something about the scope and limits of my knowledge about what is good for me in the longer term and what I ought to do.

Thinking on my past decisions and how they turned out, I know that I regret some actions and I have no hesitation in saying that I now know that they were bad for me. The extra drink that gave me such a headache and the carelessness about checking the schedule that caused me to miss my train were mistakes. Correspondingly, I know that some prudential actions that I undertook were good for me. Deciding to hide my passport in the refrigerator when I went on holiday turned out to be a good decision when thieves ransacked the house and took all my other legal and financial documents. Visiting the dentist regularly has reduced painful episodes of toothache.

I can assert with confidence statements such as:

1) 'Because I was careless in looking up the timetable, I missed my train, which was bad for me.'

2) 'Because I was prudent in hiding my passport in the refrigerator, I escaped its being robbed, which was good for me.'

But what about 'acts and omissions' undertaken on a grander scale, for example, the decision to attend University X or to move to city Y? Can I assert with confidence statements such as:

3) 'Because I attended University X rather than University Z, my life has gone worse than it would have otherwise.'

4) 'Because I moved to city Y rather than to city W, everything has gone better for me than it would have had I moved to W.'

Here I am rather doubtful. I may have certain beliefs or even 'convictions' about these propositions, but I don't think I can really know how my life would have gone had I attended University Z or moved to city W instead.

One reason for being sceptical about my power to evaluate claims like 3) and 4) is that I find in myself a tendency to rationalise by finding something 'good' even in events and decisions that had regrettable aspects. Had I never broken my back in a riding accident, I would never have read all of Kant's *Critique of Pure Reason*. Had I not taken up with P who broke my heart, I would not have learned so much about chamber music. Some good things come out of some misfortunes, and some misfortunes come out of good things, and the chain of causes can extend over a lifetime. Imagine that my broken heart (bad for me) causes me to learn a great deal about chamber music (good for me), which causes me to be hit by a bus on my way to a concert (bad for me). Or that by becoming immobilised (bad for me), I become enchanted with Kant's *Critique of Pure Reason* (good for me), and as a result spend my life writing incompetent commentaries on it and dying in ignominy (bad for me). So was it good for me or bad for me that I took up with P or broke my back? The question seems undecidable.

The thought about the past, 'Event E was good for me' implies that 'If E had not happened, things would have been in some respects worse for me, and they would not have been overall better for me.' But how can I know this to be the case? What would otherwise have happened to me in the long run would have depended on a lot else besides the non-occurrence of E. I cannot factor in these other events associated with the non-occurrence of E. For it was E that happened, and I have a sense of what did follow from E. But I can only guess at what would have followed from E's not occurring.

Should I suppose, nevertheless, that all events that have happened to me—including so-and-so becoming Prime Minister in my lifetime and such and such cosmic rays striking me—are either good for me, or bad for me, or indifferent, though for most of these events, I can never know which? This seems a fantastic supposition. I can imagine a very capable biographer who writes the story of my life in such a way that the various good, bad, and indifferent effects of various events are brought out. But such a biography, if it were not to be both incredibly long and incoherent to the average reader, would have to be highly selective in treating only 'major' events and their 'significant' impacts. It would be open to the objection of critics that for any event E whose value for me is discussed in the book, if E had not happened, the effects portrayed as flowing from E might have happened anyway, so that certain effects alleged to be good or bad for me were not really due to E. These considerations lead me to doubt that I or anyone else can have a thorough and complete understanding of what is good or has been good for me, regardless of the satisfying and plausible autobiographical and biographical 'stories' that can be constructed, portraying certain decisions as wise or foolish. The 'acts' involved in 3) and 4) and their effects are so complex compared to the 'acts' involved in 1) and 2) and their effects, that it seems there is no objective fact of the matter, knowable by me or not.

I have not lost my conviction that with respect to 1) and 2) I can judge wisdom and foolishness correctly. Nevertheless, this complexity and the fact that simple cases like 1) and 2) shade gradually into complex cases like 3) and 4) may have implications for the problem of moral knowledge.

In any case, life presents me with constant opportunities for decisions, decisions that I must take consciously or that will turn out to have been taken by default. These decisions, when acted upon, change the probabilities of certain events occurring in the future. So I must constantly decide what it is best to do for my own well-being. In making decisions about my self-interest, I need to ignore unlikely possibilities such as a pile of gold falling from the ceiling or amazing good luck in escaping disaster, and I cannot look too far into the future. It is accordingly sensible to pay attention to likelihoods. Deciding to go to medical school increases the chances that I will become a practicing physician from close to, though not quite, 0% (I might decide to practice medicine without a license) in case I don't go, to perhaps 50% if I do go. (Not all who go to medical school finish the course, and not all who finish the course become practicing physicians.) Deciding to marry X rather than Y reduces the chances that I will ever visit China from around 95%, in case Y is a patriotic Chinese with many affectionate relatives, to some lower figure in case X is not. Few of my ordinary decisions, however, have outcomes that can be predicted with certainty, and even to estimate the likelihood of one outcome rather than another, I need access to statistics that may be hard to come by.

It occurs to me that good practical decisions are not the same as decisions that will maximise my pleasures and minimise my pains. If, for example, I could attach myself to a machine that stimulated the pleasure centres of my brain on an ongoing basis, I would not consider it in my self-interest to do so. Nor would I think it in my self-interest to become addicted to a euphoria-inducing drug, even if it could be reliably supplied to me at no cost. Other people may disagree; they may be in no doubt that being hooked up to an ecstasy machine would be good for them, but so what? For me, living an interesting human life, being spared certain tragedies such as losing my children, or being sent to prison, or finding myself in the middle of a war, or suffering a painful and debilitating medical condition, or being professionally disgraced, or being friendless and ignorant about the world, would be good, and I ought to do what is conducive to this end. Nevertheless, pain and boredom are not experiences I think it would be best wholly to avoid, even if I could knock out my pain receptors or take an excitement-producing pill whenever my interest in the environment flagged. For one thing, I think I learn through painful experiences about what is and isn't in my self-interest. I do, however, want my pains to be treatable and not indefinitely prolonged.

I do not always know what I ought to do and what will be good for me, but I know that I sometimes feel regret over what I earlier decided to do and subsequently did, and that regret is an unpleasant emotion that I ought to try to avoid. I ought to be at least somewhat prudent, for the prudent person is less apt to suffer regret over their former stupidity, haste, and carelessness. However I do not think I ought to be as cautious as possible. For it is possible to be too dedicated to minimising regret—so dedicated that one misses out on a good deal of pleasure and excitement. Exactly how cautious I ought to be and how thoughtless, hasty, and careless I may be without negatively affecting my welfare is a problem I cannot solve. I can only seek out information about likelihoods and try to put it to use, taking into account my individual, indeed unique nature.

So let me consider a typical decision: the frugality vs. pleasure dilemma. Here is what I know about my situation:

The most attractive flat available costs 30% more than a minimally acceptable 'baseline' flat.

If I choose the most attractive flat, there is a very good chance that I will run out of funds by the end of the year, whereas the baseline flat is easily affordable.

I am very likely to survive, to need a flat, and to be able to enjoy a flat until the end of the year.

All these assumptions involve likelihoods. My existence might be cut short in the next instant, or I might not require a flat if I wind up in the hospital for a very long stay. I might inherit money from a long-lost relative and have no more financial worries. My tastes in flats might change. All of these eventualities are possible, and my choice of the more or less expensive flat would turn out to be fortunate or unfortunate depending on which were realized. But they are unlikely. On the basis of what usually happens, I might reasonably decide that it is prudent to take the less expensive flat. If it matters to me a great deal to live in a very nice flat, however, I might reasonably decide to take the risk of running out of funds. Taking the baseline flat could be a bad decision if I were miserable there and if I would gain quite a bit more enjoyment from a nicer flat, even if the financial risk is greater.

Now suppose that a range of 100 flats is available at various rents, their attractiveness varying with their prices, and their prices corresponding to their riskiness for me. Is there a fact of the matter about which flat it is best to take? Can I come to know which one is best? Could it be the case that, whatever I decide to do, there was an 'optimal flat' that balanced attractiveness against risk, assigning to each value the weight it ought to have? Some people doubtless believe that there is just such a unique flat. God, they might think, is omniscient, so God must know which is the optimal flat for me (as well as which University, X or Y, would have been better for me in the long run to attend). For every possible decision I could take in a situation, they think, there is ranking of the alternatives, so that one is best, one is worst, and the other alternatives are all better or worse than one another, but worse than the best and better than the worst. Even if I lack the information and concern required to work out what would be good for me, there is an objective fact of the matter—dependent on my likings and dislikings, but objective nevertheless.

This seems a peculiar assumption. Either there is an omniscient God or there isn't. If there isn't an omniscient God, there is no being who, by definition, must know which is the unique optimal flat and how all the others stack up. Even if there is an omniscient God, this God can only know everything there is to be known. I am not persuaded that the identity of the optimal flat and the ranking of the other 99 flats is one of the things to be known. Even if these are things an omniscient being can know, I think they might nevertheless be forever beyond human reason just as certain colour or tone discriminations lie outside human perception.

Rather, it seems to me that amongst the 100, there might be a range of flats such that it is definitely reasonable for me to take one of them; another two ranges of flats, all of which would be definitely unreasonable for me to take because they are either too expensive or too unattractive; and a lot of flats that do not definitely belong to any of those categories. Whichever flat I decide on, I may have regrets depending on how things turn out; I may regret spending so much, or not spending more. But if I made my decision—whatever it is—by pondering the risks and rewards for a reasonable length of time, I will at least not be able to accuse myself of having been foolish and impulsive, however things turn out. I will not reproach myself for having acted unwisely, even if I bemoan my living conditions.

Practical reasoning of this sort is, then, strongly dependent on probabilities and on the information I have about myself and about the world. Where my practical decisions are concerned—Shall I marry P or Q or nobody? Change jobs and cities or stay where I am? Buy a car or forego the purchase?—I must take into account facts about what usually happens to the average person in my situation, facts about how I am different from the average person, and consider the likelihoods of various outcomes for me.

But can I ever really know what I *ought* to do in my own self-interest—what is *good* for me or *better than* the alternatives? Can I ever be sure that I have figured that out? Consider the following two accounts of what I did:

1) I did what seemed to me most reasonable in light of what I actually knew and cared about.

2) I did what was most reasonable in light of what I ought to have known and ought to have cared about.

I can be reasonably certain that I have fulfilled the conditions of 1). Suppose I decided to smoke. I had no data on the long-term harmful effects of smoking and I liked to smoke. The decision seemed to me altogether reasonable. But it is hard to see that I acted on the basis of my *knowledge* that it was in my self-interest to smoke.

By contrast, if I was able at the time to fulfil the conditions of 2) it seems I would have succeeded in acting in my self-interest. But it seems impossible for me to know that I have fulfilled those conditions. There are many things I *wish* I had known before I took certain decisions, but the class of things I *ought* to have known is different, and poorly demarcated.

On prudential grounds, I ought to know what's on the label of the medicines I take and whether the local weather forecast is for tornadoes if they are common and devastating around here. Such well-known dangers as overdoses and harmful drug interactions are made known by Cultural Transmission and I am responsible for being alert to them.

More problematic is the second clause. Can the culture really settle what *I* ought to care about? Why should I care about things I don't? On reflection, I can see that this makes sense. I may not care that my drinking water is heavily contaminated with arsenic, but it is definitely in my self-interest to care about this. If I care about my health, I ought to care to some extent about my diet, my drinking water, the effects of privatisation on cleaning practices in hospital wards, and other such matters, and to seek out factual information about these things even if Cultural Transmission is not providing it.

So, the claim that I ought to do what I would do if I knew what I ought to know and cared about what I ought to care about seems right. But what use is it in making decisions about what to do? It is always possible that I don't know something or care about something that I ought to. And it seems that any decision procedure for deciding what I ought to do depends for its reliability on further 'oughts'—moreover, on further oughts for which the decision procedure could only involve reference to even further oughts!

This situation persuades me that no decision-procedure is guaranteed to issue in a decision that I never come to regard as having not been in my self-interest after all. In choosing a flat, I may come to realise that I did not know about some of its features or care sufficiently about others. Rather than despairing over the lack of a guaranteed method of making correct decisions, however, I can take the ineliminability of 'oughts' as an invitation always to press my reasonings and concerns as far as I can, asking myself whether I know enough to make a decision and whether I am attaching sufficient weight to the right things. I can see that there are pathways to extending both my knowledge and my regions of concern in ways they ought to be extended. I often become aware of my ignorance of certain important matters, realising that they are relevant to my condition and that knowledge is available. And I am often made aware that I ought to care about something to which I previously gave no attention—that my shoelaces were untied or that I hurt someone's feelings with my brusqueness. There is, it seems, a horizon, towards which I can extend both my factual knowledge and my concerns. But the domain of what I ought to know is limited by the knowledge that is actually available in my culture—I cannot get very far beyond what others know and can communicate to me, and I cannot extend my concerns very far outside the range of concerns other people present to me.

Armed then with the confidence that, with due diligence, I can make good decisions about what it is in my self-interest to do, I shall try to determine what else I can establish about my knowledge of 'oughts.' Can I know what *you* ought to do, what would be good for you? Or is my evaluative knowledge limited to my own case?

Here it seems to me that I am not always in a worse position in judging what it would be best for you and for other people to do in your and their own self-interest than I am in my own case. The same facts about the world and about the average person are relevant to my case and to yours. When I see you stumbling around, I know that it would be good for you to find your lost glasses. If I see that you are starving, I know that it would be good for you to get something to eat. The basis of my confidence is the knowledge that the average, psychologically healthy person has preferences to be warm, dry, well-fed, just as I do, and able to see, hear, and move around, whilst recognising that even where these basic human needs are concerned, preferences and likings may be quite variable.

For example, if you enjoy adventure travel and love camping on glaciers and catching your own food, your requirements for creature comforts are much less than those of a constitutionally or temperamentally more delicate person. You may know facts about yourself and how you are different from the average person that have a bearing on what it is reasonable for you to do in your self-interest. But I too can know these facts about how you differ from the average person, enabling me to know what you ought to do and what will be best for you. And sometimes it is the case that your emotions blind you to certain facts about how the world works and about likelihoods that are apparent to me as a detached observer. I may know that relevant information is available and even know what it is; you may not. In some cases, I am a better judge than you about what you ought to do, whereas in other cases you are a better judge than I am about what you ought to do. There is no hard and fast rule here that I can see.

So far I have considered whether I can know what it is good for me to do and good for you to do—what is in my self-interest or in yours. The good outcomes envisioned concern comfort, security, flexibility, and enjoyment and often involve trade-offs. Prudential decisions about saving, for example, concern the balance between enjoyment in vigorous youth and security in frail old age. Prudential decisions about marriage concern the balance between the attractiveness and charm of the proposed partner and their dependability and willingness to pitch in. These are all matters for investigation. Suppose I enjoy smoking but am aware that it shortens life and degrades health. How do I weigh present my enjoyment against the possibility of future misery and gnawing regret? I should consult the statistics. What condition are people usually in after they have smoked for twenty, thirty, or forty years? Have I any reason to believe that things will go differently for me? What about the people who have quit smoking? Have I reason to believe that the pleasure they formerly derived from smoking was any less than mine? Do they miss the habit so strongly that their quality of life is diminished?

In principle, I have concluded, knowledge of evaluative properties—the goodness or badness of decisions taken and actions performed by me and by others—is at least possible. Nevertheless, this knowledge is limited. It is false that for every decision I face there is a right answer about what I ought to do and a number of wrong answers. The knowledge of the world and of likelihoods and the knowledge of how I am like or unlike other people that would be required to make a reasonable decision may be unavailable to me, even if I strive to extend my knowledge and concerns to a reasonable degree. I think I should be content with the conclusion that I do *sometimes* know what you, or I, or we ought to do. I have gained, it seems to me, the right to claim that I have evaluative knowledge, but only by way of keeping my aspirations to knowledge modest.

But what about moral oughts? Judging what I ought morally to do, what it would be morally good or right to do, is not the same as judging what it is in my self-interest to do. Prudential decisions concern me, or some entity with which I identify, such as my family, or my business, or my career. If I act imprudently, then, in the absence of good luck, things will likely turn out badly for me or for one of those entities, and if I act prudently, then, in the absence of bad luck, things will likely turn out well for me or for one of those entities with which I identify. Moral decisions, though, do not seem to concern *my* security, comfort, and enjoyment—my self-interest—or at least not in the same way. A prudential decision that serves my interests could very well be one that makes me morally uneasy.

A moral ought, it now occurs to me, involves a decision about how I ought to behave towards *you* in certain types of situation or, more generally, how Person 1 ought to behave towards Person 2 in certain types of situation. I am aware that there are people who think that there are moral issues involved in how people treat or regard animals, landscapes, exotic languages, institutions like marriage or democracy, or perhaps even disused typefaces. And some people even think there are immoral ways to treat yourself. Perhaps they are right, but I suspect these views concern extensions of the central idea of morality. So I will confine myself for the present to thinking about situations involving two separate but interacting persons as morally basic. Accordingly, to discover whether there are actions, situations, events, and persons that are morally good or bad, and actions I ought to perform, or may perform, or should refrain from performing, I should investigate whether there is anything I can establish about how Person 1 ought to behave towards Person 2 when they come to stand in some sort of relationship.

Enquiry V

The Enquirer discovers that she knows some of the 'Norms of Civility' dictating how Person 1 ought to behave towards Person 2 in certain typical situations and wonders why these norms are observed and whether it is always good to observe them.

I have established that I can know a few things about what is good for me and what I ought to do for my own sake. I have also discovered that arriving at reasonable decisions about what to do in my own self-interest under conditions of uncertainty requires attention both to actual features of the world and of myself and to scrutiny of my own cares and concerns for their appropriateness.

Whenever I have to make a decision about a practical matter of self-interest—because 'doing nothing' is tantamount to making a decision—I ought to do what is reasonable even when I do not know *exactly* what is most reasonable—e.g. paying £X/pw for a flat as opposed to £X + £1/pw. To decide what to do, I ought to seek out information about what usually happens in situations like mine and to people like me when various alternative courses of action are pursued. I have to interrogate myself as to whether I have as much factual information as I need to make a reasonable decision and whether I care about the things I ought to care about. This introduces an element of indeterminacy—any decision can be regretted. Still, it would be absurd to say that no one can ever make a good decision about what it is in their self-interest to do. Further, good prudential decisions are not maximally cautious decisions. It is surely worth risking some degree of regret in case there is a reasonable chance of things working out in my interest. For I may also regret not having acted more boldly and not having taken on more risk. And some regret may be irrational, just as guilt can be irrational.

 http://dx.doi.org/10.11647/OBP.0087.05

My reasoning has also persuaded me that I can know a few things about what is good for other people and what they ought to do for their own sakes. Most people who care about their health and appearance (though perhaps not all) should quit smoking. Most people ought to save for the future and extricate themselves from intimate relationships with people who do not care about them. Accordingly, when I declare, knowing that my friend James is seriously near-sighted, that 'James ought to get glasses,' adding that doing so will enable him to enjoy films more, I am not simply expressing a certain feeling I have when I think about James's optical situation. I am not merely holding up a placard expressing my preference for James to get glasses. I am also expressing my understanding of a causal relationship between enjoying films and good vision and my knowledge of how James likes to spend his evenings. Of course James might get glasses and then discover that he is not really as keen on the cinema as he formerly thought. Or perhaps, after he gets glasses, the film industry might deteriorate seriously, and there would be no more good films to see. But I think I can still claim to know what James ought to do. It can be an evaluative fact that it would be good for James to get glasses, a fact that glasses will be good for James.

But can I ever know, not how I or someone else ought to proceed in order to make things better for themselves, but how Person 1 ought to treat Person 2? If I can sometimes know this in the general case, I can know, at least sometimes, how I, as Person 1, ought to treat Person 2, when Person 2 and I are in a certain types of situation in which normative questions about what ought to be done, or what it is right or wrong to do, arise. Perhaps I can even know how I ought to treat Person 2 in morally significant situations. But as I am not sure at this stage what a 'morally significant' situation is, I shall postpone consideration of that question.

It occurs to me that I do know certain things of this type. For example, I maintain that I know that:

> If Person 1, who is lost in a large city, politely asks Person 2 the way to the nearest bus stop, and if Person 2 knows the answer and is not in a desperate hurry on account of some pressing business or some emergency, Person 2 ought to tell Person 1 the way to the nearest bus stop.

Failure to answer Person 1's question on the part of Person 2 would be 'unkind' or 'rude.' If I were Person 1, I would be affronted if I had good reason to believe that Person 2 knew the answer to my question and was brushing me off. I would experience the brush off as a violation of what might be called an 'ought of civility' or a 'Norm of Civility.' I hesitate to say that it would be a violation of a a 'ought of morality' or of a Norm of Morality as I have not yet decided what morality is all about. Yet this Norm of Civility may have some relation to moral oughts, as reflected in the phrase 'manners and morals' and the Latin term *mores* covering customs in general.[10] So, pressing onwards, here are some further Norms of Civility that I think I know:

> If Person 1 is a guest in Person 2's house, then, upon departure, Person 1 ought to thank Person 2 for entertaining and feeding them.

> If Person 1 is a guest in Person 2's house and it is late and Person 2 begins to yawn, Person 1 ought to go home.

Further, it seems to me that I can lay down the following as general truths about how things 'ought to go' in Host-Guest situations when Guest comes to a meal prepared by Host:

> Host ought to show appreciation for Guest's coming to visit.

> Host ought to try to ensure that Guest has an enjoyable meal in comfortable surroundings.

> Guest ought to try to entertain and amuse Host.

> Guest ought to show appreciation for Host's efforts.

Perhaps just to be on the safe side, I should put 'normally' or 'usually' after the main verbs in each sentence, as I can imagine some exceptions to these generalisations. *Normally*, Guest should show appreciation for Host's efforts.

It seems to me in any case that I know all these things, and that I was taught them or learned them by watching the behaviour of other people and the effects it had. Knowing that Host and Guest ought to do these things seems tantamount to knowing how to behave as a Host or a Guest.

Where the Norms of Civility are concerned, there seems to be a great deal of room both for local convention and for improvisation. Local convention and time of day will determine whether Host should offer Guest a cup of coffee, a cup of tea, or an alcoholic drink. The ways in which Guest tries to entertain Host will depend on Guest's imagination, recent experiences, and sense of humour. Host will typically devote some thought to coming up with an interesting menu, which will usually contain ingredients that are mostly recognizable to Guest. Snake or snails will usually be on the menu only if Host is fairly certain of Guest's enjoyment of these delicacies.

Other situations in which Person 1 and Person 2 interact require the intelligent appreciation of Person 2's likely state of mind and needs if the Norms of Civility are to be observed. Take the Strangers on a Train (or these days, the Strangers on a Plane) situation. How ought a seatmate to be treated? This seems to depend on many factors—the ages of Person 1 and Person 2, the difference in their ages, their apparent receptivity to conversation, and their overall state of mind—relaxed or tense. If Person 2 pulls out a sheaf of papers and begins to study them intently, it is a violation of the Norms of Civility for Person 1 to begin to ask Person 2 personal questions. If there is severe turbulence in the air and Person 2 appears distressed, it is civil for Person 1 to say something reassuring. If Person 1 finds Person 2 attractive and wants to start up a conversation and Person 2 pulls out a novel Person 1 has recently read, it is not uncivil for Person 1 to comment briefly on the book.

The Norms of Civility accordingly reflect the needs, desires, and states of mind of Persons 1 and 2. The response of Person 2 to Person 1's overture will reflect Person 2's grasp of Person 1's intentions and assessment of them. There are 'scripts' but also deviations from them. Sometimes a violation of a Norm of Civility such as asking nosy questions or interrupting someone's concentration on a task will be resented and a rebuff issued; at other times, it will be tolerated.

It occurs to me in this connection that when I initially decided to doubt all my evaluative beliefs, I did not consider that I knew *how to do* certain things in addition to knowing *that* certain things were the case. I believed that I knew how to rewire a lamp, how to make a cake, how to fill in a tax return. I also believed that I knew how not to do certain things—the 'wrong way' to rewire a lamp by attaching the green ground wire to one of the poles, and the 'wrong way' to bake a cake, namely at 220°C. I thought I could distinguish between a well-baked, tasty, elegant cake and a burnt, underdone, tasteless, or shapeless one. So when setting all my evaluative beliefs aside, I should have doubted that I knew how to do anything properly, correctly, elegantly, or efficiently, and that anyone else knew how to do anything properly, correctly, elegantly, or efficiently either. I should have supposed that we merely have the feeling or impression that we know how to do things as they should be done or are best done.

However, the assumption that no one really knows how to do anything well seems implausible. I get constant feedback from the world that tells me whether I know how to do something and how to do it well. My constantly falling off and scraping my knees is information that I do not know how to ride a bicycle, or not well. My receiving a bad electric shock is information that I do not know how to do simple home wiring. My shoelaces constantly coming undone is information that I do not know how to choose shoes or shoelaces or how to tie good knots. By contrast, if I know how to ride a bicycle, I can cycle everywhere speedily without mishap. If I know how to bake a cake, I will likely receive compliments on my baking. This negative and positive feedback convinces me of what I do and do not know how to do.

A grasp of the Norms of Civility implies the knowledge of how to do certain things, mainly in one-to-one encounters. The personal interactions involved are rule-governed but somewhat flexible 'practices'—games of a sort. I can take personal satisfaction in the exercise of skill—social polish—in much the same way as I can take satisfaction in having mastered and being able to apply the rules of chess and poker. I am aware that I have mastered these roles somewhat imperfectly; my manners are not altogether smooth, and I make blunders from time to time, as I observe others do. There are norms I cannot be expected to have mastered. I do not know how to behave with perfect correctness as a guest in the home of a Chinese family.

Knowing how to behave civilly towards others, it occurs to me, involves feedback mechanisms, both positive and negative, that are analogous to the feedback I receive in attempting other practical tasks. By mastering the norms, I am able to participate in the common forms of human life, and to receive the rewards of sociability and avoid the misery of social exclusion and the pain of criticism. The way others treat me should persuade me that I know or do not know how to behave as a guest in my local culture or in some other culture. If I go as a Guest to a dinner party in my own city and sit like a stick the entire evening, I may never be invited back. If as a Host my food is carelessly prepared and not very tasty, my further invitations may be declined. So it is that I slowly learn the norms of civility and how to behave when I am Person 1 or Person 2. My expectations of how Person 1 ought to behave towards me are formed as well, and I become puzzled or annoyed if they are unfulfilled.

I can nevertheless ask myself 'What reason do I have to adhere to the Norms of Civility? Why play the games, why master these rules at all?

Am I not free to fail to show appreciation as Guest, or provide good food as Host, or do any of the other things that Hosts and Guests ought to do, such as leaving when my Host appears tired?' For these things will cost me some effort: good food is expensive and takes time and trouble to prepare. Perhaps the evening went badly, and I did not enjoy Host's presence; it will be emotionally difficult as Guest to show appreciation.

I need to distinguish, however, between two very different questions:

1) Why ought I to conform to any Norm of Civility ever?

2) Why, in this particular case, ought I to conform to this particular Norm of Civility?

The first question did not occur to me in connection with the norms of self-interest. I didn't have to wonder why I should *ever* do what it is in my interest to do. However, where question 1 is concerned, I believe there are some exceptional people whose life situation is such that they have no reason to confirm to any Norms of Civility, ever, and they are not motivated to conform either. Such people have no desire ever to play such roles as Stranger on a Train or Host and Guest. They see no point in mastering the routines required. If I am a Happy Hermit, content with my own society and perhaps that of my domestic animals and the wildlife around me, there is no reason for me to learn and practice the Norms of Civility. If I am an Unhappy Hermit who, on account of madness or some grave psychological condition, is unable to master them, there would seem to be no point in my trying to do so because I could not possibly succeed.

The second question, however, did occur to me in connection with the norms of self-interest. The fact that something is in my interest to do can help to explain why I ought to do it, and it normally constitutes a reason in favour of my doing it. However, there may be things it is in my self-interest to do that I ought not to do.[11] Filching and lying can be advantageous to my interests if they are performed undetectably. As a postman or postwoman, I could decide to bin a small parcel at the nearest bus stop rather than walking through a cold rain to deliver it. The reasons I can cite to myself for doing things need not be decisive reasons and they may or may not be associated with motivations to do the thing. For a reason to do something can co-exist with many reasons *not* to do it, and with conflicting motivations, such as the feeling that it would be disgraceful to bin an inconvenient parcel.

I can think of several reasons why I might disregard the usual rules of Host-Guest behaviour in a particular case or be unable to live up to them.

Imagine that as Host, I have just received some terrible news and am so distracted that I fail to look after my Guests. Or that as Guest, I find that I have been invited to the home of a sadist who embarrasses and ridicules me for the first hour. I would be justified in departing abruptly and without thanks. Or maybe I am a gauche ten year old who has not yet learned how to behave. If I never take public transportation, I may never have learned the conventional behaviour of Strangers on a Train, and I don't need to know it.

Or what if I simply think a norm is stupid and inconvenient? Suppose I just hate writing thank-you letters for birthday presents and believe such letters to be frequently insincere, though I know it is expected of me in my culture? Suppose I just don't do it. There is a risk that people will stop giving me birthday presents, or reproach me with ingratitude, but I may be willing to assume that risk.

I may know or believe that I can get away with unconventional behaviour. Perhaps people are loving and forgiving and will give me birthday presents anyway. Perhaps I am such a celebrity that people will perform the Guest or Host role to my benefit despite my performing my part abysmally. As a Great Man, I might sit like a stick all evening, refusing to be drawn into conversation, either because I am shy or because I have contempt for the others and know that my presence will be prized no matter what I do. Or if I am a Spectacular Beauty and Wit, I might decide to violate the Norms of Civility by interrupting the work of the busy stranger next to me in case I find him or her intriguing and attractive. I am taking the risk of a serious rebuff, but it might be one I have decided is worth it. In all of these cases, my behaviour is explicable.

The Shy Great Man, I think, has not rejected the norms of Host-Guest behaviour—he is simply incapable of living up to them. His behaviour is neither reasonable nor unreasonable. By contrast, the Arrogant Great Man and the Spectacular Beauty and Wit have calculated the likelihood of social punishment and decided to go ahead. The Arrogant Great Man derives personal satisfaction from his arrogance and Spectacular Wit and Beauty hopes for a bit of flirtation. Their norm-violating behaviour does not strike me as 'irrational,' and perhaps not even as 'unreasonable' But it can be 'annoying' and carries some risk.

So the answer to question 2, why I should conform to particular Norms of Civility on particular occasions, even when there is some reason not to do so, can, I think, take one of the following forms:

Because I can avoid risk, annoyance, and social punishment by living up to the norm

Because I am able to live up to the norm without much trouble

Because the other person is playing their part appropriately

If none of these things is the case, I have no reason, it seems to me, to observe a Norm of Civility, though I may do so out of habit.

So far, then, I have established that in human life there are certain conventions dictating how Person 1 ought to behave towards Person 2 when they are occupying particular social roles and that there are reasons for observing them. I learn these norms through practice, imitation, instruction, and social feedback. Other people's mastery of these norms may be different from mine. And the particular forms these conventions take will vary from society to society: burping shows appreciation for a meal in some cultures; in others it is considered rude. A thank-you note or a telephone call may be expected or not expected after a visit, etc. But insofar as I am neither a Happy Hermit nor an Unhappy Hermit, I am satisfied that there are things I ought to do that are different from those that are directly in my self-interest. I think I have established that:

1) There are ways that Hosts and Guests or Strangers on a Train ought and ought not to behave whenever they encounter one another. These are the Norms of Civility.

2) The reason for someone to act in accordance with Norms of Civility in general is that it is generally rewarding and easy to take part in human society, though a Happy Hermit may find satisfaction outside of it, and an Unhappy Hermit might be incapable of participating.

3) There can nevertheless be a good reason to disregard a particular Norm of Civility in a particular case.

I can therefore be confident that there are good reasons to observe the Norms of Civility whenever there are no special reasons not to do so. My social life will be made easier and more pleasant if I do than if I don't. To understand the nature of the 'oughts' of self-interest, I had to consider such notions as: 'needs,' 'comforts,' 'bad outcomes,' 'likelihoods,' 'available knowledge,' and 'reasonable concerns.' To understand the nature of the Norms of Civility, I have to consider such notions as: 'practices,' 'skills,' 'social roles,' 'social rewards and punishments,' 'the expectations of others,' and 'hermits.'

I no longer suppose that my beliefs that there are things I ought to do and states of affairs that are better for me have arisen only because I have been brainwashed by the warning placards waved by others, who were coerced in turn by placards written and waved about *merely* because someone else felt strongly about them and wanted others to conform. But how shall I apply what I have discovered to morality? Morality, like civility, appears to concern relations between Person 1 and Person 2. At least this is how I understood it when I decided to assume a sceptical posture towards morality. At the same time, moral relations strike me as rather different from the formal relations of Host-Guest manners. And there are at least three reasons why morality might be very different from civility.

For one thing, I appreciate that the Norms of Civility are local. Knowing how to behave in my home city does not ensure that I know how to behave in other countries, or other regions, or other subcultures. What is appropriate there, such as the Host's apologising about the poor quality of the food, or burping on the part of the appreciative Guest, may not be so here and vice-versa. Further, there is no reason for me to learn and to conform to the Norms of Civility of another culture or subculture if I do not interact with its members and have no aspirations to do so. Conformity is optional and depends on my curiosity, my interest in getting along in the culture, or my needing to do so.

The way I have always thought of morality before I decided to doubt everything was that morality was universal and applied to everyone regardless of their culture or region. Morals, I thought, involved a higher form of 'ought' than manners, and they were not optional. Whether to conform to morality, I thought, didn't depend on whether I was interested in participating in the morality system or needed to do so to avoid being ostracised. So perhaps I need to rethink this old assumption. Perhaps morals are relative to times, places, cultures, and subcultures and are optional. Or perhaps morality really does have the features I naively supposed it to and is different from manners.

A second feature that puzzles me in thinking about how the norms of civility might be like or unlike the norms of morality is the role of experts. There are experts in manners who write books and columns about how to behave in polite society. I can pretty much take their word for it about what is strictly correct in many sorts of interactions. Of course sometimes the experts admit that there is no established norm, or they suggest a new norm. The presence of former spouses at weddings is a question about a Norm of Civility. Fifty years ago, it would have been considered atrocious taste and very bad manners to issue or to accept such an invitation. Today some people might think it rude to exclude a former spouse from the guest list. But I don't see morality as working in the same way, with experts telling us exactly how to behave in a range of concrete situations. Can moral experts suggest new moral norms and put their weight behind them?

A third feature that concerns me is that the reasons I have identified for acting in accord with particular Norms of Civility, and for respecting the Norms of Civility of my Culture in general, were based on the relative lack of effort required and the rewards and satisfactions for me of mastering the skills involved. But morality, as I formerly understood it, is not a system of rules that is easy and pleasurable to master; indeed, it can be painful and detrimental to my self-interest to act morally. It will not be so easy, I fear, to find reasons for observing the Norms of Morality, either in the general or in the particular case.

I will defer these questions until I have arrived at a better understanding of what makes an interaction between two people morally significant.

Enquiry VI

The Enquirer determines what makes a relationship between Person 1 and Person 2 morally significant and investigates the origins of her moral feelings and attitudes. She then discovers that prudence and self-interest sometimes have a moral dimension insofar as they concern the relations between a Present Self and a Future Self.

Thus far I have established that I can obtain knowledge of several kinds of 'oughts'—knowledge of what is good for me and so what I ought and ought not to do, knowledge of what is likely good for others—what it is in *their* self-interest to do and not to do, and, finally, knowledge of how to treat others in a civil fashion and what to expect from them. I know how in many contexts, including some contexts in which Person 1 and Person 2 stand in conventional social roles, you and I, or Person 1 and Person 2, ought to behave, and what we ought to do and say.

My knowledge of what is good and bad for me has been acquired by observation, introspection, and through my reading and inferring. While these processes required me to have a functioning Neurological Constitution and to be subject to Cultural Transmission, there is a lot that I simply figured out for myself. I haven't only been brainwashed by my culture or forced to think things by my brain. I have taken an active role in learning about prudence and civility.

I learned early on that shocks and falls were bad for me, and I came to realise that there were many discomforts and deprivations that I preferred to avoid. My life went better when I was warm, dry, amused, occupied with meaningful work, had the companionship of interesting people, access to books and films and natural landscapes, such as fields, forests, lakes, and oceans, and when I could take pleasure in clothes and furnishings. All these things made my life better in the sense that it was more pleasing to me. To the extent that I am a typical person and others are like me, I can assume

 http://dx.doi.org/10.11647/OBP.0087.06

that what's good for me is good for them as well, and I can therefore claim to know that they ought to strive for and to have these things. To the extent that I recognise others as having different preferences, abilities, and limitations, I can know what is good for them and what they ought to strive for and have, even if these goods are not those that I ought to strive for and to have.

In turn, my knowledge of how to behave in civil fashion was acquired by instruction, observation, and social feedback. I grew up in a culture, I was told what to do, I experienced the approval and disapproval of my fellows, and I experienced resentment and gratitude at the incivility and civility of others. I established that I could ignore what I had learned only if I was prepared to be a Happy or forced to be an Unhappy Hermit, for if I were to try to behave consistently like an Arrogant Great Man, I might save myself the effort of civility for a time, but only until others became fed up with my behaviour and excluded me. Moreover, I continue to learn how to treat Person 2 and how to expect Person 2 to treat me as new situations with different relations and conventions arise and I continue to refine my knowledge and correct my behaviour.

To return to the central question, what is 'morality' all about, if it is different from self-interest, prudence, and civility?

Reflecting back on the kinds of issues I used to consider 'moral issues,' before I decided to put all my moral beliefs in question, I recall that they clustered around a certain range of topics amongst which were: bodily harm and killing, treatment of the young, the helpless or vulnerable, the actions generated by love, passion, and sexual attraction or repulsion, deception, economic exploitation, and damage to a person's self-esteem, confidence, honour, or reputation. What do these topics have in common, I now wonder? What has sex to do with killing, or financial behaviour with insult?

Let me try to recall some of the actions that, before I decided to question all my moral ideas along with all my other normative ideas, I considered morally wrong. I still have not established that I can *know* them to be so, but here are some that occur to me:

1) A politician poisons a political rival.

2) A police officer tortures a prisoner to make them confess.

3) A woman tells a man the falsehood that she is pregnant to persuade him to marry her.

4) A man who has been living with a woman refuses to take a paternity test to establish whether he is the father of a woman's child.

5) A student writes and sells essays to other students.

6) A mother chains her young child to the bedpost to go to a nightclub.

7) An employer profits magnificently by forcing his employees to work long hours for low pay.

Like violations of the Norms of Civility, these situations involve the purported misbehaviour of Person 1 towards Person (or sometimes Persons) 2. But what do these situations have in common in virtue of which I used to regard them as violations of morality?

Reflecting on what these cases have in common, I can see that the actions performed by Person 1 are deliberate[12] in every case, and that they fulfil a personal desire, ambition, or goal of Person 1 at the expense of Person 2. The 'helping' behaviour of the student in 5) certainly benefits the lazy or untalented purchaser in the short run; it can only be wrong if it harms the purchaser in the long run because they do not learn, or if it harms those who had to write their own essays, or misleads future employers. The politician believes they will benefit from having their rival out of the way; the police officer that they will obtain valuable information which it is their mission to obtain; the woman seeks the security of marriage; the man, escape from a financial burden; the student desires more spending money for desired goods; the mother, an exciting evening out; and the employer, profit.

In cases 1 and 2, the cost to Person 2 is death, or extreme pain and grievous bodily harm. In case 3, the cost is entrapment in a relationship; in 4, it is disappointment—perhaps abandonment and humiliation; in 5, the loss of due reward for effort and ability in a competitive situation. In 6, Person 2 is immobilised and risks physical injury and psychological distress; in 7, Person 2 experiences exhaustion and poverty.

Now, I do not think that there is anything unreasonable as such about the desires of Person 1 in each of the cases above when they are considered 'in the abstract.' Political victory, obtaining a confession to a crime, security, sex, spending money, and profit are all legitimate human aims. Their pursuit makes the world go round. But even worthy aims can impose costs, hardships, and suffering, just as deliberate cruelty and sadism do.

So 'morality,' I think, is essentially the subject that deals with relations between Person 1 and Person 2, where the satisfaction of human aims that impose costs on others is concerned. (Perhaps one can behave morally and immorally as well towards animals, or the landscape, or the ocean, or even towards oneself, but I think it is important to get clarity on moral relations between different persons first.) Insofar as morality concerns the behaviour of Person 1 and Person 2 in certain familiar types of situation in which they are interacting, it is like civility. But morality also concerns the prudential interests of both Person 1 and Person 2. For I think I can see that:

> In pursuing her prudential interests—what's good for her, her self-interest— Person 1 can undermine the prudential interests of Person 2—what's good for him.

What about actions of the sort I used to consider morally worthy before putting everything in question? The following occur to me:

1) A politician resigns his post to care for his recently disabled wife.

2) A police officer intervenes to stop a colleague from manhandling a prisoner.

3) A woman tells a family-oriented man who is getting serious about her that she is unable to bear children.

4) A man assumes financial responsibility for a child born outside of wedlock and helps to care for it.

5) A teenager takes a wallet full of cash they found on the bus to the police without removing any of it.

6) A mother works long hours to pay for art supplies for her talented child.

7) An employer responds promptly and effectively to an employee grievance.

In each of these cases, Person 1 gives up something that is normally valued in order to benefit Person 2 or prevent a harm to Person 2. The politician gives up fortune, fame, and influence; the police officer, the chance to obtain valuable information; the new father, a proportion of his time and income. The woman may lose a man she loves; the teenager foregoes a windfall; the mother sacrifices her free time and recreation; and the employer may reduce his profits by improving working conditions. Yet, these are the sorts of actions I was formerly inclined to think of as morally good.

At the same time, I was never disposed to regard any and all actions intended to prevent harm to or to benefit another person as moral. I recognised cases in which Person 1 could make things better for Person 2, but without acting morally. For example, I can imagine cases such as the following:

1) A show-off tipper leaves a waiter a 50% tip to impress their companion.

2) A driver speeds up on the motorway when entering from the slip road so that other drivers need not anxiously brake.

3) A father leaves his desk and rushes to comfort his child who has fallen and skinned their knee.

4) A politician puts their career at risk by voting for a law that lowers the tax rate for top income earners.

In these cases, Person 1 confers a benefit on Person 2 (or on several Persons) that requires something from Person 1: money, attentiveness, interruption of a project, or the sacrifice of popularity. However, the intention of the tipper is not to sacrifice for the benefit of the waiter, the driver simply follows the rules of good driving, and the father acts spontaneously and irresistibly. In Case 4, political effort was required, and the action was bold and risky, but the wealthy beneficiaries are perhaps not deserving of the benefit, and the side-effects of the politician's action for the poor may be deplorable. The fact that an action is done only in order to show off, or from good manners, or from an unreflective impulse, or only benefited someone incidentally—someone who did not really deserve it—seems to disqualify it as a moral action. A quintessentially moral action, on my former understanding, is one that is done at a cost to the agent that he or she recognises, that goes beyond everyday good manners or caretaking, and that is done reflectively, with the intention of benefiting someone. But wouldn't this characterisation fit the underling Person 1 who risks a long prison term by helping the Mafia boss Person 2 to fit concrete shoes on their victim? It must also be the case, I suppose, that the benefit conferred does not contribute to the harm that is done to yet another Person.

Further, there seem to be certain kinds of harms Person 1 can inflict on Person 2 for Person 1's benefit that, although they are extremely serious, I had trouble conceiving as quintessentially immoral. For example:

1) A brain-damaged man kidnaps and murders five young women.

2) In a fit of rage, a normally forgiving and equable woman stabs her taunting, unfaithful husband.

3) A schizophrenic patient leaps from a window to his death, devastating his family and deeply upsetting the hospital staff.

The results of these actions are terrible—the suffering they cause to Person 2 or a number of affected persons is immense and irreparable. Yet the 'benefit' Person 1 receives is not the sort of benefit that the agents in my earlier cases received. It is not obvious to me that the actions of Person 1 are under control in the same way as the earlier cases described. The brain-damaged killer is driven by a neurological abnormality; the two others act out of desperation or from disturbed states of mind. To say that they act 'immorally' seems both too weak, given the horror of their deeds, and too strong, given their inability to engage in the sorts of knowing and caring that would deter them from these deeds. The realm of morality thus seemed to me to embrace deeds that present constant temptations to normal people—people who are persuadable rather than compulsive.

Morality, like civility, seems to depend on the existence of social relationships, even relationships that are not mediated by language. It is not surprising to me that Darwin thought that all social animals that can help one another to survive and that are capable of interfering in the lives of others of their species might be able to evolve a form of morality. In my own case, the fact of my social dependency on other humans has long been obvious to me. Without these others I could not survive, or, if I did survive, I would not resemble a human being of the sort that lives in any culture. I have read reports of feral children, fed by animals of other species, who grew up mute and unaccustomed to the care and teaching of a mother and other adults and to interaction with other children. They behave very strangely, and I can readily believe that to grow up in a culture and to participate in observation, imitation, and conversation with other humans is absolutely necessary to becoming a normal human being.

The desire for human society in babies, for example, is not instilled by life in human society, or not altogether, while, at the same time, experience in human society is needed to become human. True, there are hermits who turn their back on human society and live in caves or in the desert, but I have reason to believe that they are either suffering from a type of mental illness or have been so inspired by devotion to an idea or an ideal that they have adopted a form of life that most human beings would find distressing and unsustainable. This is not to say that some degree of solitude is not good for me. I am surely able by my very nature to tolerate and even to enjoy periods when I am alone with my work or my thoughts.

But why do I prefer to live in a society with others rather than on my own? Why is it in my interest to do so? When I was young, I could not nourish myself and depended on others to feed me; as a young child unable to swim, run fast, or make judgements about invisible dangers, I was unaware of the threats posed by animals or violent human beings, by fast moving automobiles, electric currents, poisons, and water. I required tending when sick, and, were it not for the care of my elders, I surely would not have survived my infancy. As an older child, I required to be shown what plants and animals were edible and how to procure and prepare them, how to fashion and use tools to do so, and how to build or find shelters against cold or wind or heat. I imagine that for my ancestors these methods of instruction were quite different, as they are for people living in different cultures today. In my own country, I do not learn how to build a hut and thatch the roof but rather certain intricacies having to do with buying or renting houses or flats, and keeping them in good repair, which I rely on others to explain to me. I depend on others for amusement and entertainment with jokes and stories; they can do better at this than I can myself.

Further, I depend upon others to explain to me what to expect from my own behaviour and that of other people. I do not need to be taught when someone is angry, for I can interpret the raised voice, the flushing, the scowling as threatening to me, but I need to be taught why people sometimes become angry when I cannot see the cause for it, and when I am perhaps myself the cause.

I can see now that from the dependency of my ancestors on others for nourishment, for protection from danger, and for learning, my own dependencies, however different in form, have persisted and arisen. I must find a mate and co-operate with that person to produce and raise to maturity our offspring, and I can understand the origins of romantic obsession, jealousy, rejection, and other forms of human behaviour as efforts to attract and retain the best mate I can.

I need not be in doubt that certain of the things I judge to be good for me—the nutritional and environmental requisites of life and a surrounding society—really are so and that this is the case in view of the way I came to possess enjoyment in these things and a desire for them through a long process of evolution.

In particular, I seem to share a narrower set of dispositions with my closer evolutionary relatives, the apes and monkeys. I suppose that there was a common ancestor and that this explains the similarity between the faces and bodies of apes and mine, though we also differ in the upright gait, the differentiation between hands and feet, the larger brains, and the relative hairlessness of my species.

Apes, I have learned, share food when others beg for it. They may threaten one another and even injure one another, but they generally do not kill other members of their local troops. They assist one another by grooming and tending one another's wounds and show concern when a member of their party is injured. Some animals appear to grieve over the deaths of their fellows and to remember them. I seem to have inherited some of these patterns of behaviour. Like my living primate relatives, I have the capacity to make friends, to display loyalty, to seek revenge and to suffer it, and to be helpful to others, especially those who have been helpful to me.

But some dispositions, I have learned, are specific to my species: for example, spontaneous food-sharing, paternal care of infants and children, elaborate ceremonies for the dead, the veneration of ancestors, and religiosity. The fact that my species employs articulated language with a complex grammar, and that thoughts can be memorised and recorded on paper, that they can be discussed and debated, gives rise to practices that the other animals cannot share in. I have learned as well that there are powerful human capabilities including 'mind-reading,' the ability to understand what others feel, believe, and do or do not know. At the same time, much of people's inner lives is hidden from me.

What I perceive as a good or bad condition of the world can motivate me to take action. If I notice a picture hanging crookedly on the wall, I tend to want to straighten it. If I see that the refrigerator door is open, I move to shut it. If someone asks me to remove a splinter or examine a wound, I am quick to do so. Many of my 'corrective' reactions of this sort seem to have to do with harm to others. I notice the following:

1) When I observe a child about to run into a street full of cars, I am immediately inclined to stop her.

2) When I observe someone getting a bump on the shins, I wince. If someone shows me an injury or begins to bleed, I start to feel a little unwell myself.[13]

3) If someone near me is struggling with a package to open a door, I am inclined to help.

4) If I read in the newspaper of the mistreatment of workers or children, I feel a sense of unease or even anger.

5) Although I know that it is not real, a film in which a young person dies or lovers are separated forever can make me weep.

These responses indicate that I know what it is like to have difficulties, to need something, to struggle with something, or to be in pain; that I am disposed to mirror the suffering of others even when they are fictional; and that I try to improve matters when it is easy to do so.

I conclude that some of my responsiveness to other's requests, and to the needs and wants I can see they have even when they are not articulated, together with some of my feelings of approval and disapproval of others' actions, are part of my inherited Normative Kit. The urge to pick up a crying baby if it is my own, to feed it, to fret over the injuries of my children, to help strangers struggling with bundles, and to give directions to those who are lost is spontaneous and must have been imprinted in my evolutionary history.

But doesn't evolution favour selfishness? I can see that this is not necessarily the case. Evolution favours whatever behaviour is conducive to my getting my genes into the next generation. Kindness and altruism may help me if others help me in turn to survive and flourish. Selfishness may induce others to withdraw their co-operation or to punish me. Helpfulness and kindness to my siblings, cousins, and my parents who share my genes are also conducive to getting my genes and those I share with my close relatives into the next generation. Moreover, anger when I have been cheated or when I observe that another is being mistreated may improve my relations with others and the social environment. With less stress, I can reproduce and bring up my young more easily.

I suppose that I am a typical human being and that others of my species have similar underlying dispositions and tendencies. I know, however, that there are persons who do not feel empathy, who are not troubled, and who are rather excited and gratified by the suffering of others.[14] They are not a threat to my project of understanding morality and its sources, but they are, I concede, a threat to peaceful and happy existence.

In this way I think I have come to a better understanding of what morality is and how moral dispositions have evolved in my species. Whenever Animal 1 could gain something for itself—food, a sexual opportunity, a good place to sit or sleep, or the intimidation of a rival, but does not take advantage of the situation so as to spare an injury to Animal 2, and whenever Animal 1 confers a benefit on Animal 2 at some cost or some trouble to itself, it is showing 'proto-moral' behaviour. Animal 1 could have gained a short-term advantage for itself by molesting, hurting, killing, deceiving, raping, or thieving from Animal 2, or refusing to help it, but it resists the impulse. These self-denying patterns of behaviour must not only have enabled the groups in which they arose to flourish, they must have enabled the more moral animals to out-reproduce the less self-denying ones. For otherwise the selfish ones would have dominated in these populations. My evaluative judgements are accordingly based in nature in the sense that nature has fashioned me into a creature spontaneously disposed to generate useful emotions and evaluations in the face of certain actions, events, situations, persons, and useful feelings of right and wrong, obligation and shame.

In order to understand the nature of the 'oughts' of self-interest, I had to consider such notions as: 'needs,' 'comforts,' 'good and bad outcomes,' and 'likelihoods.' Good decisions regarding my self-interest took these features of the world into account. To understand the 'oughts' or Norms of Civility, I had to consider such notions as: 'practices,' 'skills,' 'social roles,' and 'social harmony.' Good decisions about how to behave in a civil fashion and when to do so depended on my taking these features of the world into account. And now, in order to understand the notion of a 'moral ought' or a 'Norm of Morality,' and to make good decisions about what to think and how to behave in morally significant situations, it seems I have to consider such notions as 'sacrifice of interests,' 'reciprocity,' and perhaps even 'species-specific behaviour.'

Meanwhile, the following thought occurs to me. Morality and self-interest seem to have something in common that I did not earlier suspect. Decisions about what is in my self-interest can involve questions of sacrifice. My present self may stand to my future self in the relationship of Person 1 and Person 2.

Suppose I decide to give up smoking, which I enjoy, so as not to die prematurely, or to scrimp and save so as to avoid pauperism in old age. My Future Self has thereby extracted a sacrifice from me! Why should my Present Self sacrifice their enjoyments in order to reduce the risk of misfortune to Future Self? Why shouldn't my Future Self endure pains, if they come, so that Present Self can enjoy the moment? While some prudential dilemmas—such as whether to continue at the poker table in the hope of recouping my lost winnings or quit now—do not concern the relations between the Present Self and the Future Self, many such dilemmas do. I now realise to my astonishment that they are a kind of moral dilemma, involving an action by Person 1, my Present Self, which can benefit or harm Person 2, my Future Self.

In making prudential decisions, I take the needs and comforts of my Future Self into consideration along with those of my Present Self. It would be irrational to attach too much weight to the needs and comforts of my Future Self, for the future may never in fact arrive, or it may be shorter than I expected. But it would also be irrational to attach no importance to the future and to think only of the present moment. Who in their right mind would not act now so as to prevent their experiencing a searing, long-lasting pain ten minutes or two days from now, even if the measures required for prevention were slightly inconvenient or troublesome, or involved a lesser pain? Thus prudence requires that reasonable interests be weighed in a reasonable way. What allocation of burdens and benefits, amongst all those I can envision, do I prefer? What will my Future Self have to say about my decision?

At the same time, insofar as my Future Self does not yet exist, the decision to sacrifice now on behalf of my Future Self or, conversely, to require my Future Self to suffer deprivations for the sake of my Present Self is made from the unique perspective of Present Self, who is required imaginatively to project into the future. There are many possible futures and many possible Future Selves, making prudential decisions that concern the long term exceedingly difficult. I can, however, try to find out how people like me facing similar dilemmas to mine who have chosen one way or another come to feel about their choices. By and large do people conclude: I wish I had saved more, foregone the champagne, quit smoking? Or do they wish they had indulged themselves more and stored up more memories of good times to look back on? I can read biographies of people who seem to resemble me to get a sense of how things turned out for them or ask friends and relatives. Alas, however, I cannot get useful feedback from my Future Self—not until it is too late, at which point my story becomes a source of useful information for others.

It is often hard for me to be certain that I know now what it is in my self-interest to do, what I ought to do, and what will be best for me. Perhaps the question of whether I made the right decision regarding the allocation of burdens and benefits between my Present and my Future Self can only be answered when the future arrives, on the basis of the regret or relief I come to feel. But my aged Future Self might be unreasonably resentful of the youthful indulgences of my Present Self. Moreover, the correctness of my decision, on this view, will depend on the moment n at which I recall and evaluate it. The decision could be 'correct' by these standards at t1 but then 'incorrect' at t2 if my regrets are postponed. Furthermore, insofar as the entire purpose of prudential deliberation is to identify the right course of action *now*, it does not help me to know that I shall endorse or regret this decision at various times in the future. My conviction that my decision is a reasonable one that has taken into account all that I ought to know and all that I ought to care about will weaken as the distance between now and the time I am planning for lengthens.

Nevertheless, I conclude that I can sometimes know what I or someone else ought to do. My judgements are reasonable if they would survive scrutiny based on the considerations I arrived at earlier: what usually happens, what most people want to happen, and why I could consider myself to be an exception to the general rule, either because I want something different or because the usual outcome is less likely to happen to me.

With luck, I can arrive at reasonable decisions even if I fail to perform this scrutiny. For example, suppose I am motivated to quit smoking by seeing a public service message on TV. Responding to urgings presented on TV is a very dubious method for making good choices. Nevertheless, the decision to quit smoking is in fact reasonable if I am a person with an average risk for the debilitating diseases and the average desire to avoid them.

Enquiry VII

The Enquirer discovers an analogy between the Present Self's natural and moral concern for the Future Self and the Narrow Self's natural and moral concern for the Extended Self of kith and kin. She goes on to ponder whether she has any natural concern for Strangers and why she ought to care about them.

It now occurs to me that my self-interest is not narrowly limited to my Present Self and the array of possible Future Selves whose interests I consider in my self-interested reasoning. Some of my happiness and sadness arises from the experiences and conditions of others who are close to me, for example, my parents, siblings, children, and mate. I find in myself a strong incentive to act in their best interests and to consider their interests as continuous with my own.

As a parent, sibling, child, spouse, or as a close friend, I can consider myself in two ways, either as a Narrow Self, whose desires or interests may be at odds with those of my children, siblings, parents, spouse, or friends, or as an Extended Self, forming a unit with these others, such that their good is mine as well. In the latter case, I try to do what's good for the Extended Self. In the former case, I may have to determine whose interests—those of the Narrow Self or those of family members and friends—are to be sacrificed and by how much. In particular cases I can ignore or entirely discount the interests of these others, just as I can ignore the requirements of my Future Self, but the wholesale shrinkage of concern to the Now and to the Narrow Self would be a pathological state. Imagine a person utterly indifferent to the severe pain, dismemberment, or death they are threatened with in a week's time because they only care about Now, or a person who could watch, unmoved, torture being perpetrated on a family member. I have no doubt that such people exist, but I need not concern myself with them here. As they are beyond the reach of reason, lacking the sorts of feelings that make productive argument possible, they cannot be persuaded by philosophy.

   http://dx.doi.org/10.11647/OBP.0087.07

At the same time, I am aware that human nature is such that the interests of parents, children, siblings, and mates can come apart. Ancient history, myth, and drama illustrate the conflicts that tear families apart and the cruelties that closely related or paired persons can perpetrate on one another. The brothers Cain and Abel quarrelled with a fatal outcome. Medea killed the children she had with Jason in fury at his abandonment of her, and Agamemnon sacrificed his own daughter for a fair wind. The closer people are in familial relationships, the greater the opportunities for both care and concern and for anger and aggression. This conflict can be dramatic, as in the cases just cited, or it can exist on a familiar but troubling level. Should I loan money to my struggling but slightly lazy brother knowing it will never be repaid? May I install my aged and demented parents in a nursing home despite their protests? As there is both agreement and conflict between my Present Self and my Future Self, so there can be conflicts between my 'Narrow Self,' the present and future mind-body complex that I am, and my 'Extended Self,' the set of people and causes that I care about and with whom I identify.

A fully satisfactory resolution of the conflict between these various Selves requires attention to the welfare of all involved. It also requires that the Narrow Self and the Present Self, who are charged with deciding what to do, are sufficiently well informed to make a decision and care sufficiently about what they ought to. For example, in the case of conflict between the Now and the Future Selves, my method is to try to adopt the perspective of the not-yet-existent Future Self through imaginative projection, asking myself what it will be like to be my 45- or 50- or 87-year-old self and how I will then judge my youthful actions. I need to initiate a debate between my Now and Future Selves that draws on factual information and objective likelihoods. In the case of conflict between the Narrow and the Extended Selves, I might adopt an analogous method, projecting myself into the position of my relative or mate or close friend and initiating a debate over whose interests need to be recognised and how far. This debate too should draw as far as possible on the facts of the situation and on information about likely outcomes. However, if the Narrow Self is depraved, insane, temporarily blinded by passion, or deeply irrational, it cannot care about the things it ought to and cannot make reasonable decisions, and the Extended Self may well become a helpless victim.

Even if a Narrow Self is sane, rational, calm, and not in the grip of depraved tastes, it can make the same kinds of errors vis-à-vis the Extended Self as the Present Self can vis-à-vis the Future Self. The Present Self can weigh the interests of the putative Future Selves too heavily, giving up too much pleasure and adventure now for an only probable future, or too lightly, by weighing the interests of the Present Self too heavily. I may make corresponding errors in weighing my own individual interests against those of others about whom I care. I may err in always putting their desires and well-being before mine and thereby doing myself an injury, or in always putting my desires and my welfare before theirs.

A negligent parent risks the death or loss of a child, or their alienation and the loss of their affection. Failure to feed them or educate them will impair their chances of becoming independent. Neglected mates may vanish, and neglected elders cannot furnish advice and company. My Narrow Self may benefit from altruism directed to friends and family. But such altruism can also be harmful to it. I might devote myself to my children, becoming a bore to the adults in my life. I could become a slave to a very sick and petulant elderly parent who rightly belongs in an institution.

These considerations lead me to wonder whether the Extended Self has an interest in the good of others beyond the family and beyond the circle of friends, mates, and lovers, and if so what the source and meaning of this interest is.

There are several reasons for supposing that I have been equipped by nature with some form of general sympathy. Human beings routinely show concern for and interfere on behalf of human beings they do not know. It seems to be part of human culture to create institutions whose only purpose is to help strangers in need. These institutions range from doctors and hospitals, to police and fire services, to courts intended to secure justice and to protect the weak and victimised, by applying the same rules to rich and poor, powerful and powerless. Whether they succeed or not, whether they are corrupted or not, political bodies such as senates and councils are formed and carry out their proceedings under the assumption that their entire purpose is to do what is best for the whole community. To the extent that I approve of the existence of these institutions and am willing to support them, I must care about the good of others besides those with whom I am intimate. My wider concern is evidenced by my sense of approbation and relief when I read about the outcome of a trial that seems to me just, or the passage of a bill that I think will be good for the country or for a needy and deserving element of the population.

Further, when I see a perfect stranger about to receive a blow or about to trip and fall, I cringe, and this response seems to me automatic: no one has ever taught me to do that. The alarm and shock of bystanders at a traffic accident indicate that humans are profoundly moved by disasters that do not affect their Narrow or their Extended Selves. Indeed, I spontaneously feel anxiety and discomfort when watching an adventure film or when reading a suspenseful novel. I do not know the hero and heroine and they are not even real; yet how things turn out for them is important for me.

A third reason for believing that I have something of a natural disposition to care about Strangers is the discovery that a certain small subgroup of the population lacks this concern. Things go better for them when other people suffer at their hands. They appear to be lacking the neurological requisites that enable me and most other people to respond to suffering with aversion and a desire to help. This syndrome can also be an effect of brain damage and can be considered a serious impairment.

However, my relationship to Strangers, as well as to friends and family, is characterised by some ambivalence. Much of the time I am simply indifferent to Strangers and ignore them and their plights. And humans often relate to other humans they do not know well with fear, by assuming they are dangerous and might kill them, rob them, rape them, or exploit them.

These observations do not answer the question, 'Why *ought* I to be concerned with the well-being and sufferings of Strangers?' They rather make it salient to me that I already am to some degree and that I would have to make a special effort to become completely unconcerned with the well-being and suffering of Strangers under all circumstances. At the same time, it seems that I have to make far more of an effort to be concerned with the well-being and suffering of Strangers to anything like the same degree as the well-being and suffering of those in my immediate circle.

The demands and requests for consideration of its interests implicitly presented by my Future Self—the sacrifices it is asking for from my Present Self—come in the form of worries about the future; the ghost, as it were, of self-to-come interrogates me about my current plans and practices. To be sure, worry about the future is more common and more intense in technologically advanced societies in which there are such phenomena as careers, wealth-accumulation, pensions, and inheritances. Hunter-gatherers do not need to and cannot therefore worry about these matters, but they may well worry about health matters or the approach of death. Some individuals of the happy-go-lucky type in technologically advanced societies are little prone to worry, or only begin to worry when it is too late to affect the future. However, this individual indifference exists in a broader context of human concern wherever social institutions have made such concern possible. Once the very possibilities of careers, accumulation, and so on are presented to them in early adulthood, people tend to become concerned with their own futures. This concern intensifies as these goals present themselves as within reach. Parental lectures, career advice bureaus and placement offices, newspaper and magazine articles, messages from the bank, and literary forms such as biography and autobiography all impress on me the message that the decisions I make and actions I take now are important and necessary for the future. Those who seem not to care about their own futures are reproached, either literally or by implication, by other persons and institutions. Without these external prompts, it is unlikely that I would worry about the future or think very much about it at all.

The demands and requests to my Narrow Self presented by the relatives and intimates of the Extended Self are a different matter. These people exist now, and they are usually articulate about their desires for food, transportation, advice, financial assistance, companionship, presents, and so on. They usually present their needs and desires to me directly. The very young and the elderly, even if they do not or cannot ask for attention and assistance, usually make it obvious when they need help. All human societies provide a cultural framework in which we are urged to be aware of and attempt to some extent to meet the needs and satisfy the desires of family members, friends, and mates—advertisements for cleaning products and food items as well as advice columns about how to be a good husband or mother are examples of this urging. The natural partiality for kith and kin is thus reinforced by social mechanisms. Those who are negligent are reproached, directly and indirectly.

When it comes to the demands and requests of Strangers, however, the situation is very different. Take, for example, starving persons in sub-Saharan countries, or the unemployed in our own, or persons who might be exposed to radioactive emission or toxins in their drinking water in some distant community. They do not talk to me or appear before me, manifesting their needs and desires; they don't present their requests and demands to me with the same vivacity as my intimates do. Moreover, there are far too many needy Strangers to invite my focussed rumination on their various conditions and deprivations. Hence it is obvious from a psychological point of view why I am inclined to worry about my future and to make provisions for it, and to worry about the condition of my family and friends, but not to worry a great deal about Strangers. Whereas

I have a considerable, often 'visceral' incentive to consider the demands of my future self and my relatives and intimates, which I experience as urgent, the general human concern with Strangers exemplified in those of our institutions devoted to welfare and justice does not supply me with a strong, visceral, urgently-felt incentive.

Nevertheless, as the requests of the Future Self become manifest in complex technological societies, the needs and desires of Strangers also become manifest. I become aware of them through media reports that communicate the sufferings of people in war-torn regions, in factories and slums, and in areas ravaged by natural disasters such as earthquakes, famines and floods. I become aware of the effects of unemployment, poor health, and poor healthcare in distant communities. As a result of this awareness, the Stranger puts pressure on Me, and Strangers put pressure on Us, just as the Future Self puts pressure on the Present Self, and the Extended Self on the Narrow Self. In each case, meeting demands and requests requires sacrifices from the Present Self, the Narrow Self, or the I or We who confront the Stranger or Strangers.

Still, these observations do not answer the question, 'Why ought I to be concerned with the well-being and suffering of Strangers?' nor the question, 'How concerned ought I to be and how much should I be prepared to sacrifice my narrow interests or my extended interests on their behalf?' In trying to answer these questions, I think it might be useful to distinguish between *motives* for being concerned and *reasons* for being concerned, where a reason is a consideration that ought to be a motive whether it is or not.

Some people do respond to the knowledge that Strangers are in trouble with a strong, visceral desire to help. They feel the pressure acutely and respond to it by joining Doctors Without Borders or Habitat for Humanity, or they volunteer in schools, libraries, and prisons. But others do not. They consider charity appeals a big nuisance and immediately bin any request for donations even if it is accompanied with pictures of starving children.

There are some considerations that could be presented to a person who lacked the sympathetic dispositions just mentioned and that might persuade her to take an interest in the sufferings of Strangers. She might be reminded that she might someday want or need the assistance of Strangers in the case of an accident or a national disaster when no family member or friend is available to help.[15] It could be suggested to her that by performing acts of assistance to Strangers in need, she increases the likelihood that such help will be available to her and to her friends and family, should it ever be required. But I do not think every indifferent person will be moved by this argument. Perhaps they are well-cushioned financially, well-insured, and surrounded by loyal and powerful retainers and bodyguards. They regard it as so unlikely that they would ever require the help of Strangers that the argument does not move them. Or perhaps they could be moved by fear — the fear that it could be dangerous to their personal, narrowly-construed welfare to ignore the needs and interests of Strangers, who might turn on them resentfully or breed dangerous diseases.[16] Bringing to their attention the danger of violence or harm emanating from a set of deprived Strangers might motivate the indifferent person. But again, I do not think that this will necessarily result in their conversion to a broader form of altruism.

At this point, I might appeal to their sense of honour. I might propose to them that the character of the broadly altruistic person is noble, upright, and estimable and that the character of the indifferent person is selfish and contemptible, or that their behaviour is more characteristic of 'lower' animals than of human beings with humanity.[17] This might have some effect, especially if the argument was frequently repeated. But again, results are not guaranteed. The indifferent person might brush off these aspersions as merely verbal.

Finally, I might try appealing to the rationality of the indifferent person, rather than to their insecurities or fears or sense of honour — which they may not possess. A reason for being concerned with the welfare of Strangers is that my interests are in fact no more important than the interests of the Stranger; they only feel more important and more urgent to me.[18]

Sometimes reasons — even highly abstract reasons like this one — not only ought to motivate, but do motivate less selfish behaviour. But if they do not, there is nothing more to be said. There are persons temperamentally unsympathetic and uninterested in the lives of others, responsive only to considerations that move them emotionally, yet surrounded by a protective network of friends and family and unfazed by the threats of accidents, disasters, and rebellions. Philosophy will not be able to supply them with either reasons or motives for being concerned with the needs and comforts of Strangers that will move them to action.

Very few human beings will, I expect, fall into this category of the completely unresponsive once they have heard all the arguments. This is not to say, however, that the needs and comforts of Strangers must always take precedence over those of the Self. As there can be conflict and harmony between the Present Self and the Future Selves, and between the Narrow

Self and the Extended Self, so there can be conflict and harmony between the good of Me or Us and the good of a Stranger or a group of Strangers.

I am not one of those people inclined by nature to make large donations to charity or to engage in volunteer work. Indeed, I suspect that things would go better for me if I did not have to see gravely ill people wandering in the street, and did not have to learn anything about famines, massacres, and social injustices. I frankly doubt that things would go worse for me if I did not have to witness the suffering of others or become aware of injustice. So, why shouldn't I just make arrangements not to become aware of the demands in the first place, by immediately skipping most of the newspaper that deals with political issues and binning the charity appeals that come through the letterbox?

The strategy of evasion can, I realise, be practiced with respect to my Future Self and my Extended Self. If I enjoy smoking, I may decline to seek out information about the usual fates of smokers that will tend to spoil my pleasure, so as to avoid having to make the decision whether to be prudent or imprudent. If I don't like being asked to wash dishes at home and don't want to get into an argument with someone who thinks I am being a parasite, I can arrange to arrive home only after someone else has done them and can refuse to discuss the issue.

I do not think I am always wrong to avert my gaze from a Stranger's request for help. I cannot respond to every request without spoiling my own life. However, the essential problem of morality is: How should Person 1 treat Person 2 when the advantages to Person 1 impose burdens on Person 2? How far must Person 1 sacrifice and how much is it reasonable to require Person 2 to endure? What is it reasonable for Person 2 to ask of Person 1? If I project myself into the situation of the Stranger, as I have to project myself into the position of the Future Self to decide what it is in my self-interest to do, I will surely be persuaded that some requests they might make of me are reasonable. I ought to compromise, neither shielding myself from the knowledge of the sufferings of others that would make me indifferent to their good, nor sacrificing too much of my own good—that of my Present, Future, Narrow, and Extended Selves—to improve their condition.

Before their needs became so apparent to us, thanks to television and the other media, people who were entirely indifferent to the Stranger did not stand out, and they were not reproached by the judgemental voices of the culture. But today, someone who professes not to care at all about local poverty, conditions in overseas garment factories, global warming-induced flooding in Bangladesh, the recruitment of child soldiers in sub-Saharan

Africa, elder abuse in nursing homes, and other such harms to persons, and who would be unwilling to make any sacrifice, however small, to improve these situations, will seem as unusual as a person who is perfectly unconcerned with the welfare of his sisters, his cousins, and his aunts, or his own future well-being.

I can come to a reasonable decision about how much to sacrifice by constructing a discussion or debate, projecting myself into the role of any Stranger who might have a claim on my attention and my resources. In my inner debate, the Stranger must attempt to justify the reasonableness of her demands on me, given my interest in my needs and comforts and the many Strangers competing for my attention. I, in turn, must justify to the Stranger the level of attention and support I am willing to give her.

But can I actually know what I ought to do morally when questions of harm, help, and sacrifice arise? Can I arrive at 'correct' or 'incorrect' decisions that can be represented as statements, capable of literal truth and falsity, about what I ought to do? Consider the following:

'I ought to donate £5 per annum to Doctors Without Borders.'

The decision of how much I ought to sacrifice, in the cases of Present Self vs. Future Self and Narrow Self vs. Extended Self, is typically made on a case-by-case basis ('Shall I buy a new car or invest the money? Shall I allow my brother to live with me rent free this year?'). But the case-by-case basis is not practical when it comes to assessing the needs of Strangers, insofar as there are simply too many Strangers and too many cases, and I lack resources to make a measurable difference to more than a few causes. I would do better to decide how much of my time, effort, and money it would be reasonable to give to the entire class of Strangers, and then to pick and choose a limited number of causes from amongst those that are worthy and ignore the others. I could decide to give £5 to charity X but ignore the equally worthy charity Y, in the expectation that someone else will support charity Y but not charity X. This policy need not be inflexible in case I am suddenly moved by another appeal.

But can my decision actually represent or fail to represent what I *objectively speaking ought to do*? Could my judgement that 'I ought to give £5 per annum to Doctors Without Borders' be false, whereas 'I ought to give £20 per year to Save the Whales' be true?

I think it is plainly false that I ought to give £1,000,000 to Doctors Without Borders on behalf of Strangers, just as, in my earlier example of choosing a flat, it is plainly false that I should choose a superb flat that is guaranteed to bankrupt me and also plainly false that I should choose to live in a hovel just because it poses no financial risk to me whatsoever. However, just as I doubted that there was a single figure that produced a *uniquely true* statement when plugged for N into the sentence 'I ought to spend £N pw on a flat,' I doubt that there is a single figure that, when plugged into 'I ought to give £N to Doctors Without Borders,' makes the statement uniquely true. By contrast, the following statement seems susceptible of truth or falsity:

> 'It would be reasonable for me under my own circumstances and those of the relevant Strangers to give about £5 per annum to Doctors Without Borders, and so I ought to do so.'

as does:

> 'I ought to give £5 per annum to Doctors Without Borders.'

I am disposed, then, to regard the statements above as true.

Further, I have established that I know quite a bit about what I ought to do and ought not to do in various circumstances. It is held by most philosophers that if I *know* that P, where P is some proposition, such as 'Snow is white' or 'Tigers are carnivorous,' it must be *true* that P, i.e. that snow is white and tigers are carnivorous. So it seems that there are some evaluative truths and that I know some of the ones there are. I have not determined, however, whether I can routinely evaluate actions, situations, events, and persons for their moral worth and whether I can come to know, in every morally significant situation, what I ought to do.

Does it really make sense, I wonder, to think of some moral truths as known and others as waiting to be discovered, just as some scientific truths are already known, while others have yet to be discovered but some day will be? I think in this connection of aspects of reality that were once hidden from people. They did not know that oxygen was the principle of combustion, or that viruses were the cause of many diseases. Can aspects of moral reality be hidden from us now, as I am tempted to think they were hidden from our ancestors who chopped off people's heads, held vast retinues of slaves, tortured animals for fun, and so on? To answer these questions, I think I ought to explore what might be involved in coming to change one's moral practices and beliefs and what this might reveal about moral language and the relationship between moral statements and truths.

It occurs to me in this connection that I still have not directly addressed the question of whether moral judgements merely reflect the likings and dislikings of the persons who make them. In that case, what I am calling 'moral truths' and instances of 'moral knowledge' are not truths about the world and other people, or knowledge of what is the case outside my own head. What should I now think of the Destroyers' claim that 'I ought to give £5 to Doctors Without Borders' means 'I like the idea of giving £5 to Doctors without borders?' I think this question had better be settled before I proceed any further.

Enquiry VIII

The Enquirer returns to a consideration of the language of the Destroyers of Illusion to try to determine whether moral claims are nothing more than claims about the likings and dislikings of the person who asserts them, or nothing more than expressions of attitudes, and the issuing of invitations and commands, without any epistemic significance. She comes to the conclusion that the Destroyers lack a coherent position, and she goes on to consider how to think about moral norms and demands and the possible motives and reasons for being moral.

What should I now think about the position of the Destroyers, who maintain that all judgements of right and wrong, all evaluative language, reflect only personal likings and dislikings? In Enquiry II, I found some reasons to be dissatisfied with this position, but it remains somewhat plausible in my mind and I think it is time to subject it to detailed scrutiny According to the Destroyers, I'll suppose that the following sentence is meaningless and has no definite interpretation, unless some individual person in some particular cultural setting utters or writes it:

1) 'Vegetarianism is obligatory for good.'

To understand the sentence and to see how it functions, I need to imagine that:

2) S says (or thinks) that 'Vegetarianism is morally good.'

Does this mean that according to the Destroyers, if S were to express herself in a more literal and precise manner, she would say something like:

3) 'I really like vegetarianism and I really dislike carnivorism.'

          http://dx.doi.org/10.11647/OBP.0087.08

Or perhaps:

> 4) 'I really like vegetarianism and I would really like it if others really liked it too … and I really dislike carnivorism and the liking of some people for carnivorism.'

On this analysis, 'Vegetarianism is morally obligatory' when uttered by S is true just in case S has the likings and dislikings cited. 'Vegetarianism is morally neutral' when said by T is true just in case T has the corresponding likings and disliking. It does not follow that vegetarianism is both morally good and morally neutral because there is no interpretation of the sentence 'Vegetarianism is morally… .' It has to be interpreted in the context of some particular person's thinking or saying it.

Is this an acceptable way to understand moral clams I wonder? The following objection occurs to me. A person who asserts 'I like vegetarianism and I like other people's liking it' has made a statement about their own frame of mind. I would come to suspect that what they said was false—that they were lying or self-deceived about their own preferences—if I noticed that they ate meat with obvious enjoyment and encouraged others to order meat dishes in restaurants. I would come to believe that what they said was true if they avoided meat and reacted with some discomfort around those with hearty carnivorous appetites.

By contrast when a person asserts 'Vegetarianism is morally obligatory,' I don't think that the truth or falsity of this claim can be established by looking at their dietary habits. I don't think they are talking about themselves, what's going on in their heads, but about the world. If the claim is true, it must be so because of facts about animal suffering and human nutrition. Accordingly, I can't accept the Destroyers' interpretation of what a person means when they assert a moral claim.

The Destroyers might concede that their paraphrase does not work and that it, along with their earlier attempt to purify ordinary language, was a mistake. But they may suggest another way of understanding moral claims, not as true-or-false assertions of likings and dislikings, but as expressions of attitudes. On this view, moral claims are not true or false. Nor are they equivalent to or paraphrasable by any other form of statement.

Earlier[19] I supposed that so-called moral 'beliefs' might be like placards carried around by people committed to what was written on them. This view left me somewhat uneasy, but I had no good argument against it, and the Destroyers might now insist that the view can be developed into a viable theory that precludes the possibility of moral knowledge.

Suppose that rather than carrying visible placards stating 'War is Wrong' or 'End Factory Farming' around on posts, I carry as it were invisible placards around in my head and sometimes utter, write, hear, or read the words corresponding to them? The Destroyers may suggest that these invisible thoughts, in addition to audible and visible utterances and writings, *express* my feelings and attitudes about various people and goings-on, without communicating any information about the world or conveying any knowledge about it. The words I utter or write *invite* or even *command* my audience to share these feelings and attitudes. S might as well have shouted at me 'Never eat meat!' and T might as well have whispered to me 'Go ahead and have some meat from time to time.'

If S and T are expressing their attitudes towards meat-eating, however, and commanding or inviting me to behave in certain ways, I need to consider whether to obey the command or take up the invitation. After all, I don't need to take up every invitation or do everything someone else orders me to do. I have choices.

I could, it seems, just do whatever I felt like doing on the presentation of a moral claim expressing someone's attitude, including ignoring it. But I could also make an effort to try to determine whether I *ought to* agree with S or T and *ought to* comply with the command or accept the invitation. If someone's expression of an attitude can prompt this kind of critical reflection and further investigation of the issue which results in my changing my beliefs and practices, or maintaining them, but not just because they commanded or invited me, then moral utterances and inscriptions seem to lead us into the realm of truth and knowledge, contrary to what the Destroyers maintain.

I have plenty of reasons to distrust some of my natural inclinations and immediate reactions to presented moral claims. At times, my feelings incline me to protect the weak, to sacrifice my advantages, and, as Person 1, to improve the prospects of Person 2 when I am in a position to do so. At other times, my feelings incline me to ignore the needs of Person 2 or to act against their interests, or even to use them for my own purposes. I do not know how to decide what would be the right thing to do—when I should follow my feelings and when I should reject their guidance.

I know that self-interest and civility often require me to act against my immediate inclinations, and that conforming to their norms can be difficult or taxing. It can however be satisfying to make a prudent decision and to act on it, thereby advancing my self-interest, and it can also be satisfying to play my role as Host or Guest well. So perhaps I shall discover that morality is similar; its demands can be difficult but satisfying to fulfil. But while I now have a good idea how to determine what is prudent and imprudent and civil and uncivil, I am still somewhat in the dark about how to determine what is moral and immoral.

All cultures, I've observed, have certain prohibitions on theft, on certain kinds of sex, on hurting and killing, ignoring children, deceiving people and interfering with their autonomy and liberty. While the particular norms vary from culture to culture, in all these cases, Person 1 is prohibited from doing something to Person 2 that is considered to harm them physically or psychologically or to harm their interests for the benefit of Person 1. These common prohibitions and statements about moral propriety and impropriety I'll refer to, for the time being, as the Norms of Morality. They are expressed in claims such as the following, which hold in my culture and in many others as well:

1) If Person 1 is aware that Person 2's property is desirable and unattended, it is morally improper for Person 1 to take it without permission.

2) If Person 1 is asked a question by Person 2, it is morally proper to answer truthfully and sincerely.

3) If Person 2 irritates Person 1, it is morally improper for Person 1 to cause bodily harm or death to Person 2.

I can't remember exactly how I learned that these were some of the Norms of Morality in my culture, but I am sure that I learned them in more or less the way I learned the Norms of Civility, through instruction, social experience, and feedback. In reflecting on the various motives and reasons I might have for extending my concerns from the Present Self to the Future Self; from the Narrow Self to the Extended Self; and from the Extended Self to Strangers, I discovered that motives such as my instinct for self-preservation, my natural concern for kith and kin, sympathy for strangers, and also fear, worry, and the sense of honour might motivate me to be moral. In case I am very receptive to abstract considerations, I may be moved as well by the observation that I am actually no more important except to myself than anyone else on earth is, and that they are all more important to themselves than I am to them.

But can I decide to take the risk of being immoral or amoral? Can I opt out from morality on occasion in the same way that I can throw prudence to the winds and follow my impulses, or opt out from polite behaviour— sometimes even to make a moral point, if for example, my host makes a racist joke? This question strikes me as seriously difficult. For example, what if I decided to be a burglar, honest in my dealings with my friends, scrupulous in my sexual morality, gentle with my captives, but no respecter of private property? I can't see that this would necessarily lead to a fearful and bad life if I were an exceptionally skilled burglar who managed never to get caught and who enjoyed the risk. In this case, I'd have stepped partly, but not entirely, outside of conventional morality.

My decision to flaunt the norms of ownership would sit oddly with my preference for others not to thieve from me. I would be a beneficiary of other people's respect for the property norm but also a beneficiary of my willingness to ignore the norm.

There would be no practical impossibility in my situation, but I would be unable to give a simple, truthful Yes-or-No answer to the question, 'Do you think it is acceptable for Person 1 to steal from Person 2?' I would have to give the more complicated answer that it is acceptable for me as Person 1 to steal from Person 2 but not for me as Person 2 to be stolen from by Person 1.

But what if I do not care about being able to give a simple answer? There is nothing incoherent that I can see in the complicated answer.

This problem brings me back to the fundamental question. Why make any sacrifices of personal interest at all in the name of morality if there is no danger to me in not doing so, or only a small risk of punishment or retaliation? Reminding me of the fact that I belong to a moralistic species does not persuade me that I should not opt out when I feel safe in doing so, just as I may partially opt out of the norms of prudence and civility if there is quite a bit to be gained. Moreover, the stakes are higher. Observing the Norms of Civility usually does not require major sacrifices, and behaving prudently is by definition in my self-interest. But to be consistently moral, it is necessary to sacrifice quite a lot of personal advantage.

On reflection, I can only respond to this puzzle as follows: morality essentially involves a sacrifice of one's own interest and advantage in favour of another's. Accordingly, it is futile to look in particular cases for the direct advantage to me of remaining 'within' morality and observing the norms of truthfulness, nonaggression, respect for property, avoidance of sexual predation and so on. I cannot expect to discover a selfish motive for being unselfish that will consistently move me.

To be sure, I have various self-interested motives for generally respecting the Norms of Morality cited above. A thoroughgoing failure to respect and operate with the norms of non-interference with people and their property, truth telling, and nonaggression, will sooner or later, in nearly every case, isolate me from the benefits I receive from others and subject me, if I am not a psychopath, to the pangs of conscience. Few people—no matter how grand and arrogant—are so powerful that they can disrespect all moral norms with impunity over the long term and Arrogant Great Men must live in constant fear of displacement and punishment. A few extremely clever people might manage to live as liars, thieves, aggressors, and sexual predators, but most people will be more successful in achieving their aims and living well if they abide by at least some Norms of Morality. If I am not motivated by concern for my reputation and comfort, I ought to be, and in this regard, I have reason to conform. I don't find in myself any reason to disregard all moral norms, and I don't feel motivated to do so.

Yet I can certainly disregard some standard moral norms on particular occasions without fear of retaliation and without my conscience troubling me, and I am often motivated to disregard them. Indeed, I think it is sometimes reasonable to suspend the norm of truthfulness, or the norm of nonaggression or of respect for ownership in particular cases. There are occasions when I ought not to tell the truth when someone asks me a question, and occasions when I could reasonably resort to violence in self-defence. If a burglar asks me the combination to my safe, the 'answer truthfully' rule should be suspended. If a would-be rapist is troubling me, I ought to try to inflict bodily harm on them, and it is better to filch a pie from a windowsill than to starve. Sometimes pursuing my own advantage is so important to me, even if it causes harm to others, that I am tempted to say that others must simply fend for themselves. Therefore, I do not always have reason to act in accord with the Norms of Morality as they are stated above. Morality demands sacrifices, but in certain contexts, the sacrifice involved in heeding a generic norm is too great to count as *reasonable* or the benefit would go to a person who does not deserve it.

Nevertheless, there can be some *good reasons* for me to observe a particular Norms of Morality on some occasion even if I put myself at a disadvantage by doing so, and even if social punishment is unlikely to follow in case I do refuse to observe it. One good reason is that by conforming to the norm, I can avoid injuring another person (or, at least, in the case of certain moral dilemmas, minimise injury to others). Another good reason for conforming is that I thereby avoid giving anyone else a *good reason* to resent or punish me (whether or not they do resent or can punish me). People who are motivated by reasons, as we all ought to be, may well find that they are motivated by these reasons. Indeed, some people's concept of what's in their self-interest is such that they have a strong preference for avoiding harming others and avoiding being the objects of resentment. Their sense of well-being is enhanced by the conviction that they have minimised injuries to others and that as few people as possible have just cause to be angry with them. These people have, we might say, self-centred, though not exactly selfish, reasons for being unselfish.

I conclude that there are numerous reasons, many of which are likely to be motivating, for generally being moral, just as there are numerous reasons for being generally prudent and civil. Yet the Norms of Morality seem to be significantly different from the Norms of Civility. If I memorise the rules of etiquette I will rarely be stumped as to how to behave, but even if I memorise a set of rules like those above, I will often be stumped. Morality seems to concern a whole range of human interactions, often involving unique situations, whereas civility concerns stereotyped encounters between persons in fixed roles. It is all very well to say that my decisions about what to think and how to act should be based on knowing what I ought to and caring about what I ought to to the extent that I should, but how can I possibly put such abstract instruction into practice? To try to answer this question I will return to consider my earlier moral judgements, which I am still inclined to regard as correct, and their relationship to the theories of right conduct proposed by philosophers of the past.

Enquiry IX

The Enquirer ponders the question of whether there are moral truths, whether there is a method for discovering them, and what the reach and limits of moral knowledge might be. She considers in what sense there has been moral progress and an increase of moral knowledge in the world.

Before I began to doubt everything I had previously thought about morality, and came to wonder whether there were any true and false moral opinions or any moral knowledge, I made various judgements with some degree of confidence. The following actions are examples of the sort of behaviour I judged to be in most cases morally wrong:

1) An ambitious politician poisons a political rival.

2) A police officer tortures a prisoner to make them confess.

3) A woman tells a man the falsehood that she is pregnant to persuade him to marry her.

4) A man refuses to take a paternity test to establish whether he is the father of a woman's child.

5) A student writes for and sells essays to other students.

6) A mother chains her young child to the bedpost to go to a disco.

7) An employer profits magnificently by forcing his employees to work long hours for low pay.

And actions like these I judged to be in most cases morally worthy:

8) An ambitious politician resigns his post to care for his recently disabled wife.

9) A police officer intervenes to stop a colleague from manhandling a prisoner.

          http://dx.doi.org/10.11647/OBP.0087.09

10) A woman tells a family-oriented man who is getting serious about her that she is unable to bear children.

11) A man assumes financial responsibility for a child born outside of wedlock and helps to care for it.

12) A teenager takes a wallet full of cash they found on the bus to the police without removing any of it.

13) A mother works long hours to pay for art supplies for her talented child.

14) An employer responds promptly and effectively to employee grievances.

At the same time, I don't suppose my judgements to be infallible and I don't suppose that I have always known how to behave. I take it as given that I have sometimes been in the wrong morally, that I have sometimes given others decisive moral reason to resent my actions, and that I have failed to do on occasion what I ought to have done. While it is possible that I have behaved with impeccable correctness at every point, I regard this as highly unlikely. For I occasionally notice what I take to be moral failures in the people around me, and it would be a miracle if either there actually were no moral failures at all in the world or if I was unique in escaping them. So I shall suppose that I am in the wrong an average amount of the time — neither as morally good as the most saintly and self-sacrificing persons nor as morally bad as the most exploitative and selfish, but somewhere in between.

Another reason for supposing that I have sometimes been morally in the wrong is that I know myself to have often behaved imprudently, to have done things that were not in my long-term self-interest. That is to say, I privileged the needs and comforts of my Present Self at the expense of my Future Self in ways I came to recognise as wrong. Because concern for others is like concern for my Future Self, I can assume that I have often privileged the interests of my Narrow Self over the needs and comforts not only of Strangers, but even of those of my Extended Self.

If I can determine how I discovered my prudential mistakes and what led to them, I may correspondingly gain some insight into the source of my moral errors and how to prevent them. If moral knowledge involves the avoidance or the correction of moral mistakes, it may turn out to be less mysterious than I have hitherto supposed.

Reflecting on the times when I have acted imprudently, against my own best interests, I realise that these errors fall into various categories. For example:

1) Food: I have occasionally followed my appetites and later felt sick as a result of eating too much, or eating food that was too fat or too sweet, or food that, unbeknownst to me, contained some pathogen or poisonous substance.

2) Indulgences: I have felt powerfully inclined to excess—for example to drinking too much alcohol. Drinking too much has left me nauseated and hung over, regretting my actions.

3) Finance: I have been miserly when I would have derived great pleasure from a purchase and a spendthrift when the purchase was wasteful and unsatisfying.

4) Society: I have been powerfully attracted to friends who were not good for me, avoided some who probably would have been good for me, and wasted time with others. I have written letters hastily and emotionally that did much damage to my own interests.

What do these instances of misjudgement have in common that makes them different from situations where I knew what was good for me and acted accordingly?

In certain of these cases, some properties of the things with which I was interacting—foods, drinks, commodities, other people—were unknown to me. I was unable to tell from the qualities they presented to me that they were bad for me, for they had qualities that appeared to me to be very good indeed. Food seemed tasty, alcohol seemed to be having a good effect on my mood, it was agreeable to spend money and carry away my purchases, and people struck me as attractive or unattractive.

In other cases—my writing of hasty letters—the strength of my own emotions seemed to push me to an action that turned out to be harmful to my interests, though performing it felt necessary and rewarding at the time.

How can nature have made me so that I spontaneously sometimes do what is better for me but sometimes what is worse for me? How can I have survived a rigorous process of natural selection when I so often act imprudently against my self-interest?

My mistake, in all the cases I have just cited, involved being unable to see beneath the appearances, to predict the future, and to be motivated by what was in fact most likely to happen. In some cases, there was no way for me to know what was going to happen, for example, in the case of a rare pathogen infesting my food. In other cases, I could have ascertained the danger if I had had more experience, or investigated more thoroughly. If I knew all the real, underlying, hidden properties of things and people and did not react to their superficial qualities, and if I had more insight into causal relations in the world, I would reduce my prudential errors.

Yet it seems that I might know a great deal about things and people and about causal relations and yet still suffer from weakness of the will. An expert in substance abuse might, for example, drink too much at a party, despite knowing more than everyone else in attendance about the effects of alcohol. I might know very well that the letter I was going to write would not advance my cause and might cause trouble for me, yet be so angry or so flattered that I could not resist.

Reflecting on this matter, I have arrived at three explanations of my liability to misjudge what is better for me.

First, even if my world-imprinted inclinations and tendencies sometimes lead me to do what is worse for me, they facilitate my survival and reproduction most of the time, or facilitated the survival and reproduction of my ancestors. There must be a reason why strong emotions often move me to immediate action and why I try to conserve effort in other situations.

Second, some of my world-imprinted inclinations and tendencies may be the unfortunate by-products of others that are good for me. There must be a reason why my brain responds positively to intoxication—if I had a different sort of brain that did not respond in this way, I might not function as well as I do.

Third, some of my choices reflect social pressure or are made possible by my culture and upbringing. I may yield, unwisely, to my host's urging to have another glass of champagne. If I had not learned how to type and post letters I could not have written the letter that caused me to be expelled from the Club, however annoyed I felt. It was the interaction of my world-imprinted desires with the pressures of the social environment and the cultural materials at hand that brought about my misfortune in both cases.

I can draw several morals from this, recognizing that my spontaneous judgements about my own self-interest are liable to error:

First, I must become aware of and acknowledge my innate dispositions, which are the product of a long history of natural selection, consider the situations in which they mislead me, and control my appetites when experience has taught me that the outcome will be bad for me.

Second, I must become aware of how conventions, hearsay, informal opinions about what usually happens, and other people's expectations of me can assist or mislead me. I must think about how I am like or different from the average person. I must consider myself as a statistic, but also as an individual.

Can I do more than this to decide how it will be in my self-interest to act? I do not see how this is possible. Perhaps it will turn out, because of the way events unfold, that my actual decision produces more unhappiness, deprivation or regret for me, than another decision would have. But I can rarely know for sure what the other decision would have led to, or what its broad, long term effect on other people would have been. There is no fact of the matter about how the choice I did not make would have turned out and perhaps no fact of the matter as to whether I ought instead to have chosen that path.

Applying these lessons to the detection of moral error, I think I can see the way forward. Moral error is likely to result when I rely too heavily on my natural appetites and partialities, failing to consider the effects on other people, those close to me as well as distant Strangers, of giving them free reign. While these appetites and partialities may be deeply ingrained in my constitution, I can become aware of their operation in me and their harmful effects on others. It is not only my aggressive, competitive, self-seeking tendencies that I need to become aware of and to moderate but even certain built-in cognitive tendencies such as the tendency to stereotype people and to make overly hasty inferences about their intelligence, competence, or deservingness. A pernicious habit of judgement is my assumption that people by and large deserve their misfortunes; that, were they more prudent and resourceful, they would not suffer the fates they do.[20] My tendency to defer to strong, charismatic leaders and to avoid making a fuss even when I become aware of wrongdoing also creates moral failure.

All these habits and tendencies are shared with others of my species and are the main sources of our collective moral failures. They exacerbate self-centeredness and the refusal to consider seriously the position of Person 2 in morally relevant interactions. Further, moral error is likely to result to the extent that I am ignorant about the world, not only about cause and effect and the lessons of history, but about other people's needs, desires, feelings, and reactions.

It occurs to me now that before I came to doubt everything I was taught a set of rival theories, invented or discovered by the great philosophers of the past. These included Utilitarianism, Kantianism, and Virtue Theory. Embedded in their more general accounts of human nature and moral motivation were certain implied tests for evaluating proposed or completed courses of action to determine their status as morally permissible, forbidden (insofar as it is physically possible to do what is morally forbidden), obligatory, good, wrong, etc. These tests appeared to be constructed more or less as follows.

1) Utilitarianism: Contemplate the situation facing you and consider how you could act. Would one possible course of action serve better than another to increase the total amount of happiness or well-being in the world, or to decrease the total amount of pain and frustration? If you have already acted, ask yourself what the consequences of your action were in this regard.

2) Kantianism: Contemplate your situation and consider how you could act. Review the various possibilities, asking of each alternative course of action: What would it be like if everyone did this in the same situation? Could I coherently will that everyone act in this way in this situation? If you have already acted, ask yourself whether your action could have been so willed.

3) Virtue Theory: Contemplate your situation and consider how you could act or what you did. Does or did a particular course of action exemplify a virtue, such as truthfulness, fidelity, generosity, temperance, mercy, or kindness? Does or did it exemplify a vice such as greed, lust, cruelty, dishonesty, injustice?

Each of these proposed tests divides proposed and completed actions into distinct evaluative categories. Utilitarianism (of which there are many subspecies) says that actions that increase the amount of happiness or well-being in the world are morally good and ought to be performed, whilst those that increase the amount of pain and frustration in the world are morally bad and should be eschewed.[21] Kantianism says that actions that cannot be universalised are forbidden.[22] Actions whose opposites cannot be universalised are obligatory. Virtue theory says to practice virtue and avoid vice. It is conceivable that applying one of these procedures will lead me to all and only moral truths. But how could I possibly come to know that one or the other of these procedures—or some version of one or the other—is capable of delivering all and only moral truths if I cannot identify the moral truths in the first place? And if I can know which are the moral truths independently of using the theories, why should I be interested in the theories? If the theory conflicts with my own judgement about what I should or may do, directing me, for example, to torture an innocent person to produce a great social benefit, does that mean my judgement was wrong? Or does it indicate that there is something wrong with the theory?[23]

In fact, there is remarkable convergence amongst the three major classes of moral theory and a good fit with my own spontaneous judgements. The agents in cases 1–7 above all seem to manifest vices, and the agents in cases 8–14, virtues. Kantianism also seems to condemn the actions in cases 1–7 as wrong, for I would not judge it permissible for agents to behave in this way whenever they felt like it. Conversely, I would welcome the universalisation of the behaviour described in cases 8–14. The Utilitarian evaluation also matches the results of the others. In 1–7, the happiness or well-being of Person 1 is less than the suffering endured by Person 2. In 8–14, there is a small burden to the agent, Person 1, outweighed by a great benefit to Person 2. Insofar as all three theories agree with one another and are in conformity with my spontaneous judgements, I am disposed to regard my own judgements as secure and the theories as good normative theories.

There is a problem, however, with taking these good fits as conclusive evidence for the reliability of my judgements and the excellence of the moral theories. In astronomy, a good theory accounts for the observed and recorded motions of the celestial bodies and predicts future celestial appearances better than its rivals do. The theory in this case is said to be 'empirically adequate.' If a moral theory were like a scientific theory in this regard, it would prove its worth not only by agreeing with previous 'observations' such as those just cited, but by predicting new observations— my assent or dissent from various proposals about the moral qualities of my targets of appraisal. But I can see that this proposal will not vindicate the choice of a theory that gives the *right* answers to moral questions. Rather it will vindicate the choice of a theory that accurately captures and predicts my judgements about right and wrong. It will be empirically adequate as a theory of my Normative Kit, but not as a theory of Moral Reality. Isn't it possible after all both that my spontaneous judgements are wrong and that the theories that predict them are inadequate? Maybe the behaviour described in 1–7 is *really* morally good and the behaviour in 8–14 is *really* morally objectionable?

If a sceptic were to make this objection to me, I would be baffled. I would want to know what this sceptic could possibly mean by their claim that these moral judgements of mine are possibly upside down. In what sort of world could the agents in 8–14 be virtuous and those in 1–7 vicious? I should admit, however, that by adding certain embellishments to the situations as they were sketched, the moral status of the actions described would appear to me differently. I might not judge it wrong for a starving employee to filch money from the exploitative boss's desk. If the moral theories back me up on this, this should increase my confidence in them as well as in my own judgement. If, however, my judgement is at odds with them all, I shall face a dilemma without a formal solution. I must either admit that my judgement was wrong or declare the theories inadequate.

Further, despite their remarkable convergence on many cases, the three major moral theories can conflict in their pronouncements. A truthful, hence 'virtuous' declaration might add to the quantity of misery in the world. It would accordingly be proscribed by the Utilitarian. A Virtue Theorist would protest that many actions which produce more happiness than misery are morally wrong, such as cutting up one healthy person to transplant her organs into five sick people to save their lives—virtuous doctors do not do this. Which theory should I be led by, Utilitarianism or Virtue Theory? Or suppose I am wondering: 'May I lie to my mother to protect my brother?' If the Utilitarian answers 'Yes!—you may, provided the happiness produced by your doing so outweighs the distress,' but the Kantian answers 'No!—you could not will consistently that lies can be told whenever they spare a person distress,' what shall I do? The Virtue Theorist can only tell me that there is no unique answer, that I can exemplify the virtue of truthfulness or the virtue of kindness in this situation, but not both.

I conclude that none of the traditional theories can be regarded either as descriptive of Moral Reality in the way that Copernican astronomy is descriptive of our solar system, nor as offering the correct decision procedure for doing the right thing and avoiding doing the wrong thing. Rather, I should see each of them as a heuristic device that focuses my attention in a slightly different way on the costs to Person 2 of any proposed action by Person 1. When faced with a moral question, I need to adopt the Perspective of Person 2, the person who stands to suffer most for a proposed action. Is it reasonable for this person to accept what is going to be done to them? Would they regard the benefit to Person 1 as justifying their own burden?[24] I think this consideration can even block the extreme Utilitarian proposal to cut up one healthy person to save five terminal patients. Although the sacrifice is a great benefit to each of the five, it is unlikely that any one of them would agree that it would be reasonable for them to give up their life if they were healthy. It is reasonable to conclude that no healthy person is obliged to give up his life to save five terminally ill people.

As better prudential decisions reflect better knowledge and more appropriate concerns, so better moral decisions seem to reflect better epistemic and emotional conditions of decision-making. To engage in moral theorising is to evaluate critically the 'oughts' and norms that stem from other cultural sources of normativity, including prudence or self-interest, manners, custom, and conventions. As prudence requires me to learn more than I perhaps know now about the long-term consequences of various courses of action and to care more about certain things than I do now, so does morality. Moral progress, the growth of moral knowledge, depends on this process of expansion of factual knowledge, including an understanding of other people's lives and experiences, and an extension of concern.

To help to determine whether I care enough about the things I ought to care about it strikes me that it is important to attend to the grievances of others. My own reaction to moral injury—to being lied to, betrayed, abandoned, or exploited—is to complain of mistreatment, brooding over my grievance and announcing it to others, seeking acknowledgement of the wrong and an apology or compensation from the perceived offender, or even attempting to retaliate by harming my persecutor. Moral injury may also pertain to a group. 'We' may then voice our discontent or outrage, seek acknowledgement and compensation and perhaps revenge. We may seek to recruit allies to help us to press our moral grievance against the perceived offender. Since ancient times, there have been slave rebellions and sailors' mutinies, sex strikes, presentation of petitions, public demonstrations and riots in the street, picketing and work stoppage by unions, and other forms of collective action by persons who believed themselves to be victims of moral harm. Such complaint and protest situations are invitations to observers to consider or reconsider their existing values. At the same time, I have to recognise that the grievances of the complainers are not always sincere and justified, and conversely that many people suffer moral indignities and wrongs silently, either because they are afraid to protest or because they do not realise that they are being mistreated.[25]

The history of civilisation, as I reflected on it at the beginning of this enquiry, presented me with numerous examples of interactions between Person 1 and Person or Persons 2 that, knowing what we know now about people and how the world works, can confidently be judged to be wrong. Slavery, routine torture, imprisonment without trial, lynching, the abandonment of infants, the exclusion of women from the honourable professions, and the exploitation of wage labour are practices that I can now declare I know to be wrong. The fact that others have come to know these things as well has shaped some of the laws, institutions, and practices of the contemporary world.

In declaring that I *know* certain moral truths, by making claims about slavery, torture, corruption, deception, warfare, exploitation, and so on, I express the conviction that I have made the relevant factual investigations and critically examined my preferences. At the same time, I am loathe to fall into the sort of moral dogmatism that can encourage scepticism. There are many issues about which I am inclined to think one way or the other but I would not claim to know what is right and ought to be done. Are late second-trimester abortions morally permissible? Here I feel unable to determine what is the best compromise between the interests of a pregnant woman and the interests we ascribe to the foetus—what's good for it. Either one may be seen as Person 1 deriving a benefit at too great a cost to Person 2. And what if I expand my definition of morality to encompass relations not just between persons, but between persons and animals? Should animals, as it were, have to accept that they are reasonable prey for humans, or should humans renounce the benefits of meat-eating to eliminate animal suffering? Perhaps a more thorough understanding of what it is like to be a fearful pregnant woman, or a foetus, or an animal, or a naturally carnivorous human will make it clear eventually what we ought to do about abortion and meat-eating.

Some moral realists believe that there is a uniquely correct answer to all moral questions whether or not we will ever come to know it. This seems to me deeply implausible. There may simply be no fact of the matter, no moral truth to be discovered. Sometimes I can see that something ought not to be done—some institution or practice ought not to exist—whilst having no clear idea what ought to be done instead. I can recognise a badly run prison system or poor end-of-life policies, but positive knowledge eludes me: I do not know how to organise a prison system in the way in which I know how to ride a bike, or how best to manage intractable end of life pain and desperation in the way in which I know how to bake a cake. I do not even know the conditions under which it is morally acceptable to tell a lie or for one person to kill another. Perhaps someone else does know how to design a morally acceptable prison system or manage end of life difficulties in a morally good way? That is possible—but it is also possible that no one knows these things, and even that no one knows when it is morally acceptable to tell a lie or for one person to kill another. I am still uncertain whether they can be known.

In claiming to *know* (when I do claim this) the wrongness and rightness of actions, situations, events, and the moral qualities of persons, I think I am committed to the position that no further information—about people, their feelings, or how the world works—that I could gain, nor any correction in the scope and intensity of my caring about things, will cause me to reverse my judgement. But isn't it always theoretically possible that better information and more appropriate levels and kinds of concern would cause me to retract my judgement? I admit that this is so, yet we are entitled to make some knowledge claims even without being certain what the future will bring. I know that iron rusts in the presence of oxygen, and I am convinced that future experiences and experiments will never overturn this judgement. At the same time, I admit that it is conceivable that I and many other people are deceived about this: it is logically possible that some undiscovered element that is always bound to oxygen causes iron to rust.

I am further persuaded that, just as there is more scientific understanding in the world now than in 300 BCE, there is more moral knowledge as well. This is not to say that each individual in the world has more of each. Nor is it to say that the number of scientifically or morally false beliefs held by human beings all over the world has declined. The number of false beliefs in individual minds may actually have increased with the tremendous increase in population and with the spread of communications. Rather, to say that 'we' now know more than we did is to say that as a result of the active pursuit of scientific knowledge and moral understanding, those who have made the effort have been successful. As the world has been shaped and changed by the increase in scientific knowledge and technological expertise, it has also been changed by the increase in moral knowledge, some of which has been acquired through improvements in knowledge and values prompted by rebellion and expressions of resentment,[26] some of which through 'experiments of living'[27] that have either worked out well or have failed. This is not to say that less moral wrong overall is perpetrated now than in the past, or that the number of wrong or abhorrent moral views held by individuals has diminished. New wrongs arise as old wrongs are righted. Nevertheless, many grievous wrongs have been righted to some extent, many others are in the process of being righted, and many others that have not yet appeared may one day be recognised as wrongs and righted.

Earlier I wondered whether there was any role for moral experts. A moral expert of the most expert sort would be a person who would know the solution to any moral dilemma and whose judgements of character, of right and wrong, of what is permissible, forbidden, and obligatory not only could be absolutely relied on, but ought to be absolutely relied on. Could any human being really fulfil this role? Maybe not. At the same time, I accept it that there can be good and bad advice in matters of prudence from those whose predictive abilities and knowledge of likely outcomes are well developed. So why not suppose that there can be good and bad moral advice from people whose understanding of the biases of judgement, the conditions of life, and responses to them of persons involved in morally significant relationships are richer than mine? Their ability to imagine possible ways of restructuring those relationships in better ways would render their pronouncements superior to mine. They ought accordingly to be preferred by me to my own initial judgements, and I should investigate thoroughly the reasonings and opinions of those who appear to have thought most deeply about these matters. But it is hard to distinguish such persons from others who are quick to give advice and opinions, and in the end relying on my own considered judgement is the best way forward I can think of.

Summary

The Enquirer summarises the results of their investigation

Perturbed by the amount of moral uncertainty and disagreement in the world, the variety of practices that people accept or reject as morally proper, and puzzled by my own indecision on important moral questions, I decided to doubt what common sense had up to now appeared to tell me: that there were such things as good actions and evil intentions, virtue and vice, moral obligations and permissions, and that actions, situations, events, and persons could have moral qualities. I decided to make a clean break from the view that morality was anything real.

First, I tried out the hypothesis that nothing is really right or wrong, better or worse than anything else, and that I was under the illusion that actions, events situations and persons possessed such properties as being 'evil,' or 'morally heroic,' or 'morally forbidden' or 'morally permissible.' To enable me to entertain this supposition, I supposed that all evaluative properties are illusory. I supposed that menu items are not really 'delicious' and crocodiles are not really 'dangerous,' and that I only experience them as such because of my cerebral wiring and the beliefs and preferences impressed on me through my culture. I reminded myself that the deepest theories of the world that we possess—physics and chemistry—do not contain value judgements or terms that connote values.

However, I came to realise that I do not live amongst and experience the particles and forces of physics and chemistry, and that the world I live in unavoidably presents itself to me as value-laden. I realised that although I could at times adopt an entirely detached perspective in which neither tragedies nor happy surprises mattered, I could not do so over the longer term or as a way of life. The possibility of purging my language, not only of value terms like 'good,' 'right,' and 'obligatory,' but also terms with

http://dx.doi.org/10.11647/OBP.0087.11

connotations of value like 'film-star' and 'criminal' seemed remote. Most of my ordinary vocabulary would have had to go.

I then imagined a population of Destroyers of Illusion who had purified their discourse by interpreting all value-laden terms as reflecting the speaker's likings and dislikings, rather than as reflecting the properties of evaluated things. The Destroyers appeared to have satisfactory paraphrases for all the sorts of evaluative statements I am in the habit of making. When I said something was right or good, they translated this to mean that I said that I liked it, and when I said something was wrong or evil, they translated this to mean that I said that I disliked it.

Next, I determined that, even if the paraphrases of the Destroyers might be good translations of what I really mean in making evaluative judgements, this did not impact on my claim to know certain evaluative facts. I could after all know something about what is good and bad. The Destroyers could not convince me that I did not *know* that my existence was better than my nonexistence. Indeed, they could not convince me that I did not know certain things about what was in my self-interest and what was in the self-interest of other people. I determined, however, that knowledge about what it was in my own self-interest to do or to refrain from doing, and what it was in other people's self-interest to do or refrain from doing, was often hard to come by. Making good decisions about self-interest often depends on acquiring as much relevant factual information as possible about the self involved and its particular situation, and about what usually happens. It seemed that the best thing for me to do in my own self-interest on various occasions was what I would be motivated to do if I knew what I ought to know and cared about what I ought to care about, and that the same was true in the case of other people. For me to know how to advance my self-interest on a given occasion, I have to know as much as I need to in order to make a decision and I have to care sufficiently about the right things. But of course the claim that I know and care enough on any given occasion is itself a value judgement. It is hard to see how I could know that claim to be true. Nevertheless, the observation that the truth of a knowledge-claim about values implies the truth of these other claims gives me an incentive to seek information and to reflect critically.

I then went on to consider several ways in which people can interact with one another. I noted that I have firm expectations about the 'right way' and 'the wrong way' to behave in certain social situations according to the conventions of good manners, ordinary friendliness and decent behaviour.

To some extent, then, I and others seem to know 'how to behave.' I then speculated on the possible motives for conforming or refusing to conform to the conventions of 'good manners.' I decided that a person might often be motivated to deviate from conventions they knew about and that they might sometimes even have a good reason for deviating from these conventions. I decided that there were nevertheless good reasons to observe these conventions most of the time; it was usually in my own self-interest to do so. Hermits, by contrast—whether happy or unhappy—might have neither reasons nor motives to observe what I called the Norms of Civility.

I went on to try to determine how morality was both similar to and different from manners. Both manners and morals, I could see, involve relationships between two people or between one person or group and others. In 'civil encounters,' people confront one another in such roles as Host and Guest, or Strangers on a plane, or as tourist and native. In 'moral encounters,' people confront one other in such roles as spouses, friends, officials and constituents, parents and children, employers and employees. I determined that morality is nevertheless somewhat different from manners in several ways. First, morality seems at least sometimes to call for greater sacrifices than mannerly behaviour and to involve greater asymmetry between the moral agent and the person or people whose well-being they affect. Second, morality presents me with dilemmas that manners ordinarily do not. Third, morality does not seem to be a matter of local conventions; if people in a faraway culture want to eat with their fingers or slurp their soup noisily, I think it's 'up to them' in a way it's not 'up to them' if they want to marry off ten-year-old girls.

I then considered some explanation of how we human beings might have naturally evolved a disposition to sacrifice for the good of others. It was not difficult to explain these dispositions by considering the natural history of the species and its ancestors. Apes and monkeys engage in altruistic behaviour and seem concerned with fairness and reciprocity as do some other animals. I concluded that there is a biological platform for morality that is a requisite of the social life of the species and its perpetuation.

It occurred to me at that point that I had never settled the question whether the paraphrases of the Destroyers were adequate, so I returned to a direct consideration of that question. I realised that even if the Destroyers were right to suppose that the qualities of goodness and badness could not inhere in any target of moral appraisal, and even if their paraphrases in terms of 'likings' and 'dislikings' captured something of the meaning of moral claims when they were asserted, this still left me with the task of determining what actions, events, situations, and persons I *ought* to like and dislike. Should I like vegetarianism? Should I dislike torture under any conditions?

Answering these questions for myself to the extent that I could, did not involve consulting my inner experience or learning about anyone else's inner experience. I was never in any doubt that many of the things other people 'like' to do—persecute people of particular racial or ethnic groups, beat up homosexuals, marry off very young girls—were disliked by me, and that I disliked the fact that others liked them. This discrepancy in our feelings seemed to indicate that I or they *ought* perhaps to have different feelings. To determine whether I ought to be indifferent to or dislike other people's likings and dislikings seemed to require an investigation of the institutions themselves and the reasons for liking or disliking them. I would have to do some actual investigation of the practices and implications of vegetarianism and torture.

Returning to the question of the sacrifices that seem to be essentially involved in morality, I tried to determine why people might be motivated to make them or have reason to make them. It occurred to me that even acting in one's own self-interest, acting prudently, can involve sacrifices, namely the sacrifice of present enjoyments and comforts for one's Future Self. I decided that we have some natural incentive to be concerned with the welfare of our Future Selves, and also some natural incentive to be concerned with our kith and kin—our Extended Selves. I acknowledged nevertheless that some people do not care about anything except their own well-being at the present moment. It might be possible to motivate them by giving them incentives—by pointing out to them that they can avoid regret or punishment by sacrificing their short-term advantages in favour of another person. Or they might be motivated by being assured of reciprocity by others, or their esteem, or even by the prospect of achieving moral nobility or 'honour.' But I could find no contradiction in supposing that a person might be unmoved to care about their Future Self or their Extended Self by all arguments and considerations. Only this would be an unusual sort of person, and he or she would likely find themselves in somewhat poor condition and socially isolated.

A more difficult question was why I might be motivated to make sacrifices involving my present well-being on behalf of strangers. I noted that many human institutions, such as hospitals, police forces, and benefits bureaus exist in large societies of strangers. As individuals, we do have some instinctive concern for Strangers and are not only mannerly towards them but sometimes make large sacrifices on their behalf, as I noted at the start of my Enquiry. By and large, however, my concern for Strangers is weaker than the concern for my Future and Extended Selves. The incentives that might move a person to be less concerned with the present, or less selfish with regard to family and friends, such as avoidance of regret and avoidance of punishment, or the expectation of reciprocity, seemed to be minimal or lacking altogether.

I recognised that I might nevertheless be moved by the consideration that it is noble or honourable to be concerned with the well-being of Strangers, and by the reason that my enjoyments and my well-being are no more important in the grand scheme of things than theirs.

Then the question arose: how much ought I to sacrifice for the good of people I do not personally know? I had realised earlier that there is sometimes a good answer, but often no unique 'right answer,' to the question, 'What is it now in my self-interest to do?' I understood that the answers to questions about prudential 'oughts' are better the more they reflect my knowing what I ought to know and caring about what I ought to care about. I have reason to expect that the same is true of questions about what I ought to do in morally problematic situations regarding other people. My decisions will be better if I know what I ought to know and care about what I ought to. But—alas!—I can never be certain that I am in either condition. My claims to know what it is right to do are conjectural. Indeed there may be no fact of the matter as to how much I should sacrifice for my Future Self, or my kith and kin, or a Stranger, or how much I ought to require them to sacrifice for me. However, I determined that I could increase my chances of avoiding moral error by increasing my understanding of the world and people and by becoming aware of my own biases and irrationalities.

This led me to consider briefly the role of the traditional moral theories Utilitarianism, Kantianism and Virtue Theory. I could see the point of each of these theories: Utilitarianism directed my attention to the painful or pleasurable, welfare-reducing or -enhancing effects of actions on policies on everyone affected by them; Kantianism reminded me not to try to make exceptions for myself that I wouldn't grant to others; and Virtue Theory provided an easy-to-remember list of Person 1 traits that helped to assure good interactions with Person 2. I decided that employing these theories was helpful in reducing the chances of moral error, though no theory could be depended on always to give the right answer to the question of what should be done. I concluded finally that there has been moral progress as moral errors have been revealed and corrected since the time when the study of morality originated.

Discovering how I am linked to the world as a competent, self-interested being, a being who is at the same time a member of a sociable species, has given me insight into the origins of my moral feelings and opinions. I realise that I am descended from a long line of ancestors who survived and reproduced themselves because their beliefs and desires enabled them more successfully to find what they needed and to escape dangers. They must have evolved motivations, perceptions, and responses to frequently-encountered situations that preserved their lives and attracted the trust, co-operation, and assistance of others. So along with selfish tendencies in myself, it is no surprise that I find benevolent ones. My 'knowledge' that kindness and sincerity are virtues, and my motivation to be kind and sincere in certain situations, are, in this regard, rather like my knowledge that certain fruits are edible and my motivation to eat those fruits. The virtues might be said to lie within us, as our dietary tastes do. But mine cannot fully develop unless I grow up in a culture that points out to me the edible and the poisonous fruits and that punishes cruelty and lying and encourages the virtues of kindness and truthfulness.

Social learning accordingly plays a role in my identifying new edible fruits and in refining my motivations, so that I avoid the dangerous ones and develop a taste for the more salutary ones. Fortunately, along with tastes and inclinations, I have inherited certain evolved mechanisms for learning, for translating the raw data of experience into knowledge of an external world and its properties. Perhaps these learning-mechanisms fail at times, but they must at least have been good enough to enable my ancestors in competition with slightly differently endowed members of their species to produce me.

When I began my sceptical enquiry, I regarded my Neurological Constitution and Cultural Transmission as obstacles to obtaining moral knowledge, but my perspective has shifted. I can now appreciate how the norms I think of as general and fundamental—such as the norms of truthfulness and nonaggression—may correspond to inherited predispositions with a neurological basis, such that normally, I am inclined to speak the truth to others, and that normally, I am not as irritable as chimpanzees are and do not attack my fellow humans with the same vehemence I have observed in other primates. And where I first tended to think of Cultural Transmission as imposing arbitrary and often irrational and unnatural norms of behaviour on the members of various cultures, it now occurs to me that Cultural Transmission can also preserve and disseminate knowledge as it is won by me and by others over time.

I conclude that my initial pessimism in the face of the multiplicity of moral beliefs and cultural practices in the world was unjustified. I am no longer inclined to suppose that there is nothing at all to choose between various cultural practices and that all moral convictions are merely personal beliefs, with no one's Normative Kit better or worse than anyone else's.

Where manners are concerned, I think my motto ought to be 'When in Rome, do as the Romans.' I ought to master the Guest-Host conventions of whatever milieu I inhabit, recognizing the differences as well as the similarities between China and Rome and between Rome and New York. I ought to behave as a Host or Guest as others in my culture behave and in accordance with the norms just enunciated unless there is reason to do otherwise. I cannot translate this recommendation into morals, however. It seems to imply that if I had lived in ancient Rome, I ought to have acquired slaves, flogged them when they disobeyed, and cheered at gladiatorial shows—these being the norms of my culture. It seems to imply that the attitudes, emotions, and practices of Greek slaveholders and Roman circus-goers were those I ought to have had in that context. It seems to imply that I should learn and accept the morality of my culture. Now that I appreciate that moral norms may reflect ignorance of the facts or unreasonable biases, I see no need to regard all practices as equally good and defensible, though how much I ought to interfere with established practices is itself a moral question.

Finally I considered the possibility that there are moral experts who possess more moral knowledge than most people do, thanks to their extensive knowledge of human life and their appropriate levels of concern. Insofar as expert advice is available on many topics—how to cook well, how to travel safely and inexpensively—expert advice on how to treat other people in morally significant situations is probably available as well. But as it is difficult to identify the experts and as they often disagree with one another, I concluded that I was right to conduct my own reasonings, taking into account those who had long meditated on particular moral problems, and to try to reach expert status on the particular questions that I faced by myself.

Endnotes

1. Moses Finley, *Ancient Slavery and Modern Ideology*, 2nd edn, Princeton: Markus Wiener, 1998.

2. Early Judaism and Islam enacted prohibitions against this ancient practice.

3. John Boswell, *The Kindness of Strangers: The Abandonment of Children in Western Europe from Late Antiquity to the Renaissance*, Chicago: University of Chicago Press, 1998.

4. David Hume presents this possibility in his *Dialogues Concerning Natural Religion*, ed. Nelson Pike, Indianapolis: Bobbs-Merrill, 1970.

5. To put this in perspective, four billion pennies would fill 1520 blocks, each amounting to the size of a school bus: see http://www.kokogiak.com/megapenny/nine.asp

6. Some of the great Stoics from time to time seem to achieve this detached perspective. For example, Epictetus, *The Discourses*, ed. C. Gill, London: Everyman, 1995.

7. See John Searle, *The Construction of Social Reality*, New York: Free Press, 1995.

8. See Adam Smith on social sanctions, *Theory of Moral Sentiments*, Pt. II, 'Of Merit and Demerit.'

9. Hume claims 'Tis not contrary to reason to prefer the destruction of the whole world to the scratching of my finger.' *Treatise*, Bk II, Pt. III, § 3, p. 416. 'Reason' is here opposed to sentiment.

10. Thomas Hobbes describes manners as 'small morals,' in *Leviathan*, Ch. XI, p. 42.

11. John Broome discusses *'pro tanto'* reasons vs. 'perfect' reasons in 'Reasons,' in R. Jay Wallace, Philip Pettit, Samuel Scheffler, and Michael Smith, eds., *Reason and Value: Themes From the Moral Philosophy of Joseph Raz*, Oxford: Oxford University Press, 2004, pp. 4–28 [http://philpapers.org/rec/WALRAV].

12. I am not considering the case where a politician accidentally poisons a rival by lacing his soup with arsenic mistaken for salt. On morality and intended and unintended consequences, the 'doctrine of double effect,' see G.E.M. Anscombe, *Intention*, Cambridge, MA: Harvard University Press, 2000.

13. Adam Smith in the *Theory of Moral Sentiments* calls attention to these vicarious experiences; see note 8 above.

     http://dx.doi.org/10.11647/OBP.0087.12

14. Autism, certain types of cerebral pathology, and psychopathy influence moral responses and judgements. See Joshua D. Greene, 'The Cognitive Neuroscience of Moral Judgment,' http://www.wjh.harvard.edu/~mcl/mcl/pubs/Greene-CogNeurosciences-Chapter-Consolidated.pdf

15. Kant offers an argument like this one in the *Foundations of the Metaphysics of Morals*, IV: 423. He does not, however, frame it as a motivational argument directed to a selfish individual, but rather as a point of logic, insisting that it would be inconsistent for *all* members of a society to desire help when in need but to refuse to give it.

16. Thomas Hobbes attempted to show that fear, and a desire for security and long life, rather than love of humanity, could be the basis of social co-operation in *Leviathan*, Ch. XIV.

17. This is a popular rhetorical strategy employed by Plato, Cicero, and Kant.

18. An argument advanced by Thomas Nagel in *The Possibility of Altruism*, Princeton: Princeton University Press, 1979.

19. Enquiry II, pp. 29–31.

20. This pernicious tendency is discussed by M.J. Lerner, *The Belief in a Just World: A Fundamental Delusion*, New York: Plenum, 1980.

21. Is a Utilitarian agent always *obliged* to act so as bring about the greatest happiness within the agent's power, or does the Utilitarian agent generally strive to spread happiness and well-being and to reduce, eliminate, or alleviate pain? The first alternative seems too strong, the second too weak. Modern Consequentialist theories try to spell out more precisely the ways in which pleasure and pain are morally directive.

22. It is clear that Kantians have a special class of actions in mind. Thus 'Always give parties but never go to parties' is not universalisable, but no one would say that it is morally forbidden to behave in this way.

23. The method of 'reflective equilibrium' says that judgements are true and theories are adequate when they harmonise in this fashion. It was first proposed by John Rawls, 'Outline of a Decision Procedure for Ethics,' *Philosophical Review*, 60 (1951), pp. 177–197, reprinted in his *Collected Papers*, Cambridge, MA: Harvard University Press, 1999, pp. 1–19.

24. Tim Scanlon develops this perspective in his essay 'Contractualism and Utilitarianism,' in *Utilitarianism and Beyond*, ed. Amartya Sen and Bernard Williams, Cambridge: Cambridge University Press, 1982, pp. 103–129.

25. On realistic adaptation to circumstances vs. brainwashing, see David Zimmerman, 'Sour Grapes, Self-Abnegation and Character Building: Non-Responsibility and Responsibility for Self-Induced Preferences,' *The Monist*, 2003, pp. 220–241.

26. See Peter Railton's discussion of resistance to mistreatment in 'Moral Realism,' *Philosophical Review*, 95 (1986), pp. 163–207.

27. The term is J.S. Mill's, *On Liberty* (1859), ed. J. Gray, Oxford: Oxford University Press, 1998, p. 63.

Suggestions for further study

Enquiry I

John Locke presents a catalogue of startling human practices in his *Essay Concerning Human Understanding*, ed. P.H. Nidditch, Oxford: Clarendon, 1975, Bk I, Ch. III, § 9, pp. 70–71 [http://dx.doi.org/10.1093/actrade/9780198243861. book.1]. For a classic anthropological defence of moral relativism, see Edward Westermarck, *Ethical Relativity*, New York: Littlefield, Adams & Company, 1932. For contemporary discussion and defence see Gilbert Harman, 'Moral Relativism Defended,' *The Philosophical Review*, 84.1 (Jan. 1975), pp. 3–22 [http://dx.doi.org/10.2307/2184078], and Jesse Prinz, *The Emotional Construction of Morals*, Oxford: Oxford University Press, 2009, esp. pp. 173–214 [http://dx.doi.org/10.1093/acprof:oso/9780199571543.001.0001]. On moral scepticism see also Gilbert Harman, *The Nature of Morality: An Introduction to Ethics*, Oxford: Oxford University Press, 1977, and Richard Joyce, *The Myth of Morality*, Cambridge: Cambridge University Press, 2001, esp. Chs. I-II [http://dx.doi.org/10.1017/cbo9780511487101]. On the peculiarities of our moral judgements, see Joseph Henrich, Steven J. Heine, and Ara Norenzayan, 'The Weirdest People in the World?,' *Behavioral and Brain Sciences*, 33 (2010), pp. 61–83 [http://dx.doi.org/10.1017/s0140525x0999152x].

Enquiry II

Humans are judgemental: Adam Smith develops this point in his *Theory of Moral Sentiments* (1759), ed. Ryan Patrick Hanley, Harmondsworth: Penguin, 2009, esp. Chs. I-IV; an updated treatment of the moral sentiments is to be found in Jonathan Haidt, 'The Moral Emotions,' in R.J. Davidson, K.R. Scherer, and H.H. Goldsmith (eds.), *Handbook of Affective Sciences*, Oxford: Oxford University Press, 2003, pp. 852–870. Historically, the view that values are perceived in and attributed to actions, situations, events, and persons that do not and cannot literally possess them is associated with Hobbes, Spinoza, and Hume. See Thomas Hobbes, *Leviathan* (1651), ed. Richard Tuck, Cambridge: Cambridge University Press, 1996, p. 39; Baruch Spinoza, *Ethics* (1677), tr. and ed. E. Curley, Princeton: Princeton University Press, Bk III, Prop. 9; Prop. 39; and David Hume, *Enquiry, Enquiry Concerning the Principles*

   http://dx.doi.org/10.11647/OBP.0087.13

of Morals (1751), ed. T. Beauchamp, Oxford: Oxford University Press, 1998, esp. Pt. II, Chs. V-VIII and Appendix 1, p. 163. For the 20th-century version of 'error theory,' see J.L. Mackie, *Ethics. Inventing Right and Wrong*, New York: Penguin, 1977, Ch. I, and Richard Joyce, *The Myth of Morality*, Cambridge: Cambridge University Press, 2001 [http://dx.doi.org/10.1017/CBO9780511487101].

Enquiry III

For discussion of the fact-value, description-evaluation distinction, see Hume, *A Treatise of Human Nature*, Book III, Part 1, §1. See further Charles Stevenson, 'The Emotive Meaning of Ethical Terms,' in *Facts and Values*, New Haven: Yale University Press, 1963, pp. 10–70 and for criticism Hilary Putnam, 'The Entanglement of Fact and Value,' in *The Collapse of the Fact/Value Dichotomy and Other Essays*, Cambridge, MA: Harvard University Press, 2002, esp. pp. 34–48. For further discussion of 'thick' concepts that are both descriptive and evaluative, see Allan Gibbard and Simon Blackburn, 'Morality and Thick Concepts,' *Proceedings of the Aristotelian Society, Supplementary Volume*, 66 (1992), pp. 267–283, 285–299. For an eloquent defence of the ineliminability of values from experience, see John McDowell, 'Values and Secondary Qualities,' in *Morality and Objectivity*, ed. T. Honderich, London: Routledge & Kegan Paul, 1985, pp. 110–129. For an opposing view, see Simon Blackburn, 'Errors and the Phenomenology of Value,' in *Morality and Objectivity: A Tribute to J. L. Mackie*, ed. Ted Honderich, London: Routledge & Kegan Paul, 1985, pp. 1–22. See further David Copp, 'Realist-Expressivism: A Neglected Option for Moral Realism,' *Social Philosophy and Policy*, 18 (2001), pp. 1–43 [http://dx.doi.org/10.1017/s0265052500002880], and David Morrow, 'Moral Psychology and the "Mencian Creature",' *Philosophical Psychology*, 22 (2009), pp. 281–304 [http://dx.doi.org/10.1080/09515080902970657].

Enquiry IV

On moral decisions, see Jean-Paul Sartre, *Being and Nothingness*, tr. Hazel E. Barnes, 2nd edn, London: Routledge, 2003, esp. Pt. I, Ch. II, § 1–2. More recently, the connection between normativity and planning has been emphasised by Allan Gibbard, *Meaning and Normativity*, Oxford: Oxford University Press, 2012, esp. Ch. II [http://dx.doi.org/10.1093/acprof:oso/9780199646074.001.0001]. On the relevance for ethics of the notion of an 'Ideal Observer' who knows exactly what they ought to know and cares about exactly what they ought to care about to precisely the degree that they ought to, see Roderick Firth, 'Ethical Absolutism and the Ideal Observer,' *Philosophy and Phenomenological Research*, 12 (1952), pp. 317–345 [http://dx.doi.org/10.2307/2103988] and the response of Richard Brandt, 'The Definition of an "Ideal Observer" Theory in Ethics,' *Philosophy and Phenomenological Research*, 15 (1955), pp. 407–413 [http://dx.doi.org/10.2307/2103510].

For an important contribution to the understanding of prudential decisions, see Sharon Street, 'Constructivism about Reasons,' *Oxford Studies in Metaethics*, vol. 3, ed. Russ Shafer-Landau, Oxford: Clarendon Press, 2008, pp. 207–245. There is a vast literature on 'vagueness'—the problem of how much, exactly?—that is relevant to planning decisions. For a start, one might begin with the 'sorites paradox' or 'problem of the heap,' see http://plato.stanford.edu/entries/sorites-paradox. For a celebrated discussion of risk and reward in decisions of moral significance, see Bernard Williams, 'Moral Luck,' in *Moral Luck*, Cambridge: Cambridge University Press, 1981, pp. 20–39 [http://dx.doi.org/10.1017/CBO9781139165860].

Enquiry V

On the relations between morality and manners, see Philippa Foot, 'Morality as a System of Hypothetical Imperatives,' *The Philosophical Review*, 81 (1972), pp. 305–316 [http://dx.doi.org/10.2307/2184328]. On knowing how to do things, see Gilbert Ryle, 'Knowing How and Knowing That,' *Proceedings of the Aristotelian Society*, 46 (1945–1946), pp. 1–16. Ludwig Wittgenstein discussed 'language games' and the allied notion of 'forms of life' in his *Philosophical Investigations*, 4th edn, ed. P.M.S. Hacker, Oxford: Blackwell, 2009. The latter notion has wide application in anthropology and sociology as well as in philosophy. See, for example, Peter Winch, *The Idea of a Social Science and its Relation to Philosophy*, London: Routledge, 2007 [http://dx.doi.org/10.4324/9780203820766]. On social roles, see Erving Goffman, *The Presentation of the Self in Everyday Life*, Garden City, NJ: Doubleday Anchor, 1959. The problem of the Arrogant Great Man—a central problem in ancient Greek society—is extensively discussed by Plato, most notably in his dialogue *Gorgias* where Callicles presents his case at 832 ff. and 488b ff.; and in *Republic*, Bk I, 338b, where Thrasymachus presents his. See Plato, *Complete Works*, ed. John M. Cooper and D.M. Hutchinson, Indianapolis: Hackett, 1997.

Enquiry VI

On morality as a relation between Person 1 and Person 2, see Tim Scanlon, *What We Owe to Each Other*, Cambridge, MA: Harvard University Press, 1998; Catherine Wilson, *Moral Animals, Ideals and Constraints in Moral Theory*, Oxford: Clarendon, 2004, *passim* [http://dx.doi.org/10.1093/0199267677.001.0001]; and Stephen Darwall, *The Second-Person Standpoint*, Cambridge, MA: Harvard University Press, 2009. For an influential view of the components of human well-being that is controversial but important, see Martha Nussbaum, 'Human Functioning and Social Justice: In Defense of Aristotelian Essentialism,' *Political Theory*, 20 (1992), pp. 202–246 [http://dx.doi.org/10.1177/0090591792020002002]. On the intentional factor in human actions and accidental harms, see G.E.M. Anscombe, *Intention*, Cambridge, MA: Harvard University Press, 2000.

For discussion of whether free will is necessary for moral responsibility and whether psychopaths are morally responsible for their deeds, see Robert D. Hare, *Without Conscience: The Disturbing World of the Psychopath*, New York: The Guildford Press, 1999, and R. Jay Wallace, *Responsibility and the Moral Sentiments*, Cambridge, MA: Harvard University Press, 1994.

On the human being as a social animal, see Chares Darwin, *The Descent of Man* (1879), repr. London: Penguin, 2004, and more recently Robert Wright, *The Moral Animal: Why We Are the Way We Are*, New York: Vintage, 1994. On the proto-moral behaviour of apes, see Jessica C. Flack and Frans B.M. de Waal, 'Any Animal Whatever': Darwinian Building Blocks of Morality in Monkeys and Apes,' in Leonard D. Katz, ed., *Evolutionary Origins of Morality: Cross-Disciplinary Perspectives, Journal of Consciousness Studies*, 7 (Nos. 1 and 2), repr. Upton Pyne UK: Imprint Academic, 2000, pp. 1–29. Adam Smith in the *Theory of Moral Sentiments* calls attention to our spontaneous sympathy for others in Chs. I-IV. On the evolution of altruism, see Robert Trivers, 'The Evolution of Reciprocal Altruism,' *Quarterly Review of Biology*, 46 (1971), pp. 35–57 [http://dx.doi.org/10.1086/406755], and Philip Kitcher, 'Between Fragile Altruism and Morality: Evolution and the Emergence of Normative Guidance,' in *Evolutionary Ethics and Contemporary Biology*, ed. Giovanni Boniolo and Gabriele de Anna, Cambridge: Cambridge University Press, 2006, pp. 159–177 [http://dx.doi.org/10.1017/cbo9780511498428.011].

Enquiry VII

The problems posed by the existence and demands of the Future Self are extensively discussed by Derek Parfit in *Reasons and Persons*, Oxford: Oxford University Press, 1986, esp. Pt. III, 'Personal Identity' [http://dx.doi.org/10.1093/019824908x.001.0001]; also Bernard Williams, 'The Self and the Future,' *The Philosophical Review*, 79 (1970), pp. 161–180 [http://dx.doi.org/10.2307/2183946]. The analogy between prudence and morality was first noted by Henry Sidgwick, *The Methods of Ethics*, 5th edn, London: Macmillan, 1893, p. 418, and is pursued by Thomas Nagel in *The Possibility of Altruism*, Princeton: Princeton University Press, 1978.

The extension of concern to larger and larger units was a theme of the Stoics. See Marcus Tullius Cicero, *On Ends*, 2nd edn, tr. H. Rackham, Cambridge, MA: Harvard University Press, 1931, Bk V, § 22. See also Peter Singer, *The Expanding Circle*; Ethics, Evolution and Moral Progress Princeton: Princeton University Press, 2011. On our natural partiality to kith and kin, see Adam Smith, *Theory of Moral Sentiments*, Pt. VI, §II, Ch. I, and on the limits of concern, Susan Wolf, 'Moral Saints,' *Journal of Philosophy*, 79 (1982), pp. 419–439 [http://dx.doi.org/10.2307/2026228]. On the claim that moral indifference is sometimes justified, see Hallvard Lillehammer, *The Ethics of Indifference*, London: Routledge, 2013. Familial conflict is prominent in the dramas of the ancient playwright Euripides and is stock in modern situation comedy.

Enquiry VIII

A defence of 'emotivism,' the view that moral claims express the speaker's emotional stance, was presented by A.J. Ayer, 'Critique of Ethics and Theology,' in *Language, Truth and Logic*, New York: Dover, 1936, esp. pp. 105–112, and developed by Charles Stevenson, op. cit. On 'expressivism,' the doctrine that evaluative terms are, as Hume maintained, perceptual projections of speakers and that moral utterances express their attitudes towards states of affairs, see R.M. Hare, *The Language of Morals*, (1952) Oxford: Clarendon, 2015 [http://dx.doi.org/10.1093/0198810776.001.0001] and Simon Blackburn, *Spreading the Word*, Oxford: Oxford University Press, 1984. See also David Wiggins, 'A Sensible Subjectivism?,' in David Wiggins, *Needs, Values, Truth*, Oxford: Basil Blackwell, 1987, pp. 185–211.

For Plato's answer to the question, 'why be moral?,' phrased in terms of the intrinsic rewards available to the subject who enjoys a well-ordered moral constitution, see Plato, *Republic*, IX, 571a-592b, in *Collected Works*. For a challenging treatment of the question of whether I can opt out of morality, see Bernard Williams, *Ethics and the Limits of Philosophy*, Abingdon: Routledge, 2006, esp. Ch. X. On the important role of resentment in human moral life, see P.F. Strawson, 'Freedom and Resentment,' in *Freedom and Resentment and Other Essays*, London: Methuen, 2008, pp. 1–28 and also Allan Gibbard, *Wise Choices, Apt Feelings: A Theory of Normative Judgment*, Oxford: Clarendon, 1992, pp. 47–48. For resentment as a marker of wrongdoing, see Peter Railton, 'Moral Realism,' *The Philosophical Review*, 95 (1986), pp. 163–207 [http://dx.doi.org/10.2307/2185589].

Enquiry IX

Unconscious biases relevant to moral judgement, plans, and decisions are discussed by Richard E. Nisbett and Lee Ross, *Human Inference: Strategies and Shortcomings in Human Judgement*, Englewood Cliffs, NJ: Prentice Hall, 1980, and by Virginia Valian, *Why So Slow?*, Cambridge, MA: MIT Press, 1999.

Utilitarianism is classically ascribed to Jeremy Bentham, *The Principles of Morals and Legislation* (1789) and to J.S. Mill, *Utilitarianism* (1863); see also J.J.C. Smart and Bernard Williams, *Utilitarianism; For and Against*, Cambridge: Cambridge University Press, 1973 [http://dx.doi.org/10.1017/cbo9780511840852], and Samuel Scheffler, *The Rejection of Consequentialism: A Philosophical Investigation of the Considerations Underlying Rival Moral Conceptions*, Oxford: Oxford University Press, 1994 [http://dx.doi.org/10.1093/0198235119.001.0001]. The Universalization criterion is presented by Immanuel Kant in his *Grounding for the Metaphysics of Morals* (1785), tr. James W. Ellington, 3rd edn, Indianapolis: Hackett (1993), p. 30. For an updated Kantianism, see Christine Korsgaard, *The Sources of Normativity*, Cambridge: Cambridge University Press, 1996 [http://dx.doi.org/10.1017/cbo9780511554476], and Barbara Herman, 'The Practice of Moral Judgment,' *The Journal of Philosophy,* 82 (1985), pp. 414–436 [http://dx.doi.org/10.2307/2026397]. For Virtue Theory, see Aristotle, *Nichomachean Ethics,* tr. Terence Irwin, Indianapolis: Hackett, 1999, esp. pp. 40–66. A recent exposition is that of Rosalind Hursthouse, *On Virtue Ethics,* Oxford: Oxford University Press, 2001 [http://dx.doi.org/10.1093/0199247994.001.0001].

For an argument to the effect that moral claims represent conditions of the world that obtain or fail to obtain, see Peter Geach, 'Assertion,' *The Philosophical Review,* 74 (1965), pp. 449–465 [http://dx.doi.org/10.2307/2183123]. On the validation of moral claims, see John Mikhail, 'Universal Moral Grammar: Theory, Evidence and the Future,' *Trends in Cognitive Science,* 11 (2007), pp. 143–152 [http://dx.doi.org/10.1016/j.tics.2006.12.007]. For scepticism about the adequacy of theories and a defence of 'moral particularism,' see Jonathan Dancy. *Ethics Without Principles,* Oxford: Clarendon Press, 2004 [http://dx.doi.org/10.1093/0199270023.001.0001].

On the concept of moral progress, see Ruth Macklin, 'Moral Progress,' *Ethics,* 87 (1977), pp. 370–382 [http://dx.doi.org/10.1086/292049]; Catherine Wilson, 'Moral Progress without Moral Realism,' *Philosophical Papers,* 39 (2010), pp. 97–116 [http://dx.doi.org/10.1080/05568641003669508]; and Dale Jamieson, *Morality's Progress,* London: Oxford University Press, 2002. For defences of 'Moral Realism,' the doctrine that moral truths exist independently of human mental states and await our discovery, see Nicholas Sturgeon, 'Moral Explanations,' in *Morality, Reason and Truth,* ed. David Copp and David Zimmerman, Totowa, NJ: Rowman and Allanheld, 1985, pp. 49–78, and Russ Shafer-Landau, *Moral Realism: A Defense,* Oxford: Clarendon, 2003 [http://dx.doi.org/10.1093/0199259755.001.0001]. For critical discussion see Alex Miller, *An Introduction to Contemporary Metaethics,* Oxford: Polity, 2003, pp. 143–179.

This book need not end here...

At Open Book Publishers, we are changing the nature of the traditional academic book. The title you have just read will not be left on a library shelf, but will be accessed online by hundreds of readers each month across the globe. We make all our books free to read online so that students, researchers and members of the public who can't afford a printed edition can still have access to the same ideas as you.

Our digital publishing model also allows us to produce online supplementary material, including extra chapters, reviews, links and other digital resources. Find *Metaethics from a First Person Standpoint* on our website to access its online extras. Please check this page regularly for ongoing updates, and join the conversation by leaving your own comments:

http://www.openbookpublishers.com/isbn/9781783741984

If you enjoyed this book, and feel that research like this should be available to all readers, regardless of their income, please think about donating to us. Our company is run entirely by academics, and our publishing decisions are based on intellectual merit and public value rather than on commercial viability. We do not operate for profit and all donations, as with all other revenue we generate, will be used to finance new Open Access publications.

For further information about what we do, how to donate to OBP, additional digital material related to our titles or to order our books, please visit our website: http://www.openbookpublishers.com

You may also be interested in:

**Foundations for Moral Relativism:
Second Expanded Edition**

J. David Velleman

http://www.openbookpublishers.com/product/416

Beyond Price: Essays on Birth and Death

J. David Velleman

http://www.openbookpublishers.com/product/349

**Knowledge and the Norm of Assertion:
An Essay in Philosophical Science**

John Turri

http://www.openbookpublishers.com/product/397

Lightning Source UK Ltd.
Milton Keynes UK
UKHW020825020919
349038UK00005B/125/P